CELEBRATING GOD'S LOVE

Living into Christian Unity and Interreligious Relationships

Edited by
Donald E. Messer

D0097312

Abingdon Press
Nashville

CELEBRATING GOD'S LOVE:
LIVING INTO CHRISTIAN UNITY AND INTERRELIGIOUS
RELATIONSHIPS

Copyright © 2015 by Abingdon Press

Library of Congress Cataloging in Publication Data

Celebrating God's love : living into Christian unity and interreligious relationships / edited by Donald E. Messer.
  1 online resource.
  Description based on print version record and CIP data provided by publisher; resource not viewed.
  ISBN 978-1-5018-0951-4 (e-pub)—ISBN 978-1-5018-0950-7 (binding: pbk.)
1. Christian life—Methodist authors. 2. Church—Unity. 3. Church renewal. 4. Interdenominational cooperation. 5. United Methodist Church (U.S.)—Clergy. I. Messer, Donald E., 1941–
  BV4501.3
  287'.6--dc23

                                                                            2015014442

MANUFACTURED IN THE UNITED STATES OF AMERICA

15 16 17 18 19 20 21 22 23 24—10 9 8 7 6 5 4 3 2 1

Steve –
With deep appreciation for your fine writing and excellent service as General Secretary and Ecumenical Staff Officer of the United Methodist Church.

To

Bishop Mary Ann Swenson
Dr. Stephen J. Sidorak, Jr.
Exemplars of Ecumenism
and
Interreligious Relationships

You leave a superb legacy of accomplishments.

Mary A Swenson
Donald E Messer
Scott J Schiessworld
Youck Kang
Elaine J W Stanovsky
No Cal

CONTENTS

Contents

ACKNOWLEDGMENTS

A book focused on fostering Christian unity and interreligious relationships might appear esoteric or academic, except the issues examined are front page news and as timely as the latest television newscast. Headlines like a "Covenant and Schism in the UMC: Time to Split? The United Methodist Battle over Same Sex Marriage," "Amicable Breakup of UMC Needed, Pastor Group Says," and "Same-Gender Debate Rekindles Schism Talk," are shocking reminders that Christian unity even within United Methodism remains precious and precarious.[1] Likewise, captions in the social media declare "The Latest Religious War," "Religious Conflict Rips Through Central African Republic," "The World Council of Churches Opposes Pakistan's Blasphemy Sentence," and "At War with Islam?"[2] These banners underscore painful challenges undercutting efforts to promote and preserve interreligious relationships in the twenty-first century.

This volume neither addresses every issue or concern that needs to be faced nor attempts to provide a solution to every problem or conflict mentioned. Rather as an edited collection of essays in practical theology, it offers a framework for reflection and study by United Methodist laity, clergy, and seminarians seeking to live into our faith's commitment to ecumenism and interfaith relationships. Questions are provided at the end of each chapter to encourage dialogue as pastors and congregations use this book in group study sessions.

Appreciation is extended to the writers from around the world who contributed chapters. Their vision and voices are indispensable in understanding the biblical, historical, and theological basis for ecumenical and interreligious work. In preparing this book, the editor particularly is grateful for the support and encouragement of the leadership and staff of the Office of Christian Unity and Interreligious Relationships of The United Methodist Church, particularly the Ecumenical Officer, Bishop Mary Ann Swenson, and the Ecumenical Staff Officer, Dr. Stephen J. Sidorak, Jr. However, this is *not* an official publication of the Office of Christian Unity and Interreligious Relationships. Neither the Office nor the staff is responsible for the manuscript's contents, as the essays reflect solely the perspectives of the authors and the editor.

Special thanks are due my administrative assistant, Shawna Layman.

And once again, for the sixteenth time, my loving wife of more than fifty years, Bonnie J. Messer, needs to be thanked for enduring the writing of yet another book. Her encouragement and editing prove essential every time!

Notes

1. Amy Frykholm, "Covenant and Schism in the UMC: A Time to Split?" *The Christian Century*, April 16, 2014; Sam Hodges, "Amicable Breakup of UMC Needed, Pastor Group Says," UMNS, May 22, 2014; and Kathy Gilbert and Heather Hahn, "Same-Gender Debate Rekindles Schism Talk," UMNS, May 29, 2014.

2. See http://www.huffingtonpost.com/lance-simmens/the-latest-religious -war_b_5967576.html. http://www.religionnews.com/2013/11/21/religious -conflict-rips-central-african-republic/. http://www.dw.de/the-world-council -of-churches-opposes-pakistans-blasphemy-sentence/a-18030266 and http:// www.huffingtonpost.com/nida-khan/at-war-with-islam_b_5970766.html.

About the Authors

Warner H. Brown, Jr. is the United Methodist bishop of the San Francisco Area, Sacramento, California, having served eight years as bishop of the Denver Area. He serves as president of the United Methodist Council of Bishops for 2014–16. A native of Maryland, he holds an M.Div. from Wesley Theological Seminary in Washington, D.C. Ordained in Pennsylvania, he served churches there and in California, where he also served as conference council director.

Sudarshana Devadhar is the United Methodist bishop of the Boston Area, previously serving eight years as bishop of the New Jersey Area. A native of India, he began his ministry in the Church of South India. He holds a B.D. from United Theological College, Bangalore, India, an M.Th. from Perkins School of Theology, Dallas, Texas, and both an M.Phil. and a Ph.D. from Drew University, Madison, New Jersey.

Gaspar João Domingos is the United Methodist bishop of the West Angola Area, Luanda, Angola. He earned his bachelor's degree in theology at the Methodist Institute of Higher Education in Brazil and graduated from the Ecumenical Institute of Bossey, University of Geneva, in Switzerland. He has served as general secretary of the Angola Council of Christian Churches. He was elected to the episcopacy in Mozambique in 2000.

Adam Hamilton is senior pastor of the twenty-thousand-member Church of the Resurrection in Leawood, Kansas, the largest United Methodist church in the USA. He earned his B.A. from Oral Roberts University and an M.Div. from Perkins School of Theology. He holds two honorary degrees and received the B'nai B'rith Award in Social Ethics. A best-selling and award-winning author, he has written *Making Sense of the Bible* and *Christianity and World Religions.*

Benjamin L. Hartley is associate professor of Christian Mission and director of United Methodist Studies at Palmer Theological Seminary (The Seminary of Eastern University), King of Prussia, Pennsylvania. An ordained United Methodist clergy, he holds a Th.D. and an M.S. from Boston University. His book *Evangelicals at a Crossroads: Revivalism and Social Reform in Boston* was published in 2011.

Hee-Soo Jung is the United Methodist bishop of the Wisconsin Area. He served eight years as episcopal leader of the Chicago Area. Born in South Korea, he was the first Christian in his Confucian/ Buddhist family. He earned a number of degrees in Korea and the United States, including his Ph.D. from the University of Wisconsin-Madison. He served pastorates in California, Texas, and Wisconsin and taught at Kangnam University and Seminary in South Korea.

Gladys Mangiduyos is dean, College of Education, of Wesleyan University-Philippines, Cabanatuan City, Philippines. A deaconess in the United Methodist Philippines Central Conference, she serves on the steering committee of the Office of Christian Unity and Interreligious Relationships. A graduate of Harris Memorial College and the University of the Philippines, Diliman, she has been national president of Deaconess Service.

Donald E. Messer is global consultant for the Office of Christian Unity and Interreligious Concerns of The United Methodist Church. A South Dakota native, he is president emeritus and professor emeritus at The Iliff School of Theology, Denver, and former president of Dakota Wesleyan University. Author of sixteen books, Messer is executive director of the Center for the Church and Global AIDS in Centennial, Colorado. His M.Div. and Ph.D. are from Boston University.

Glen Alton Messer II is associate ecumenical staff officer at the United Methodist Office of Christian Unity and Interreligious Relationships, New York City, and lecturer in United Methodist history and doctrine at Yale Divinity School. He is a native of Michigan, and his M.Div. and Th.D. are from Boston University, where he served as visiting assistant professor in History of Christianity and Methodist Studies from 2007 to 2010.

Bruce R. Ough is bishop of the Dakotas-Minnesota Area. He served twelve years as episcopal leader of the Ohio West Area, after serving appointments in Iowa, Indiana, and South and North Dakota. A native of North Dakota, he earned his M.Div. from Garrett Evangelical Theological Seminary, Evanston, Illinois. He has been president of the General Board of Global Ministries, chair of the Connectional Table, and is president-elect of the Council of Bishops for 2016–18.

Stephen J. Sidorak, Jr. is ecumenical staff officer for the United Methodist Office of Christian Unity and Interreligious Relationships of the Council of Bishops, New York City. For more than twenty years, he was executive director of the Christian Conference of Connecticut. Previously he headed the Colorado Council of Churches. An ordained United Methodist elder, he holds M.Div. and M.S.T. degrees from Yale University Divinity School.

Mary Ann Swenson is ecumenical officer of the United Methodist Council of Bishops. She served twelve years as bishop of the California/Pacific Area and eight years of the Denver Area. Prior to her election to the episcopacy, she was a pastor in Washington. Currently she is vice moderator of the World Council of Churches. A native of Mississippi, she holds an M.Div. and a D.Min. from Claremont School of Theology.

Rosemarie Wenner is bishop of the Germany Episcopal Area, Frankfurt, Germany. She earned her theology degree from the United Methodist Theological Seminary in Reutlingen, Germany, and served as pastor of several congregations before becoming a district superintendent. She was the first woman elected to the United Methodist episcopacy outside the USA. From 2012 to 2014 she served as president of the United Methodist Council of Bishops.

In summary, the theological guidelines of scripture, tradition, experience, and reason lead United Methodism steadily along the ecumenical road.

Bishop William R. Cannon,
"Christian Unity: Imperatives and New Commitments,"
adopted by Council of Bishops, March 30, 1978

"I'm not praying only for them but also for those who will believe in me because of their word. I pray they will be one, Father, just as you are in me and I am in you. I pray that they also will be in us, so that the world will believe that you sent me."

John 17:20-21

CHAPTER 1

Responding to God's Call for a New Way of Living

Rosemarie Wenner,
Warner H. Brown, Jr.,
and
Bruce R. Ough

Seeking the unity of Christ's church and fostering interreligious relationships is at the heart of United Methodism. What is distinctive about our heritage and hope is our belief that all of God's children are precious, and with deep respect we seek to find ways by which we can "deepen and expand the ecumenical and interreligious ministries of The United Methodist Church."[1]

Often we affirm familiar words from the Letter of Paul to the Ephesians pleading for unity in the body of Christ. Each of us is expected "to lead a life worthy of the calling" of Christ and to do so "with all humility and gentleness, with patience, bearing with one another in love, making every effort to maintain the unity of the Spirit in the bond of peace." This calling is to "maintain," not create, unity. Unity is God's creative initiative; it is a gift of God through Christ. We are the stewards of this gift. This calling is not just personal but corporate, as we avow that "there is one body and one Spirit, just as you [are] called to the one hope of your calling, one Lord, one faith, one baptism, one God and Father of all, who is above all and through all and in all" (Ephesians 4:1-6 NRSV).

BREAKING FROM PAST PATHS

We seek to respond to God's call for a new way of living that breaks dramatically from past paths that too often have prized divisiveness and championed schism and separation rather than unity and relationships. When we remember our own church history, we are painfully aware of past splits, often because of racism, regionalism, and tribalism. We know that even today healing and reconciliation still are urgently needed.

When we look globally, we recall how too often people of differing religious perspectives and persuasions have become alienated from one another and how families and communities have been devastated because of religious misunderstandings and misdeeds. Seeking and maintaining Christian unity and interreligious relationships are not options, but theological obligations of our faith because we affirm a God of love and follow Jesus, the Christ, who transcended narrowness of spirit and always pressed for greater inclusivity.

The ecumenical movement of the twentieth century sought to shatter the exclusiveness and barriers Christians often erected by doctrines, polities, practices, prejudices, and institutions. The rigidity of boundaries between persons of different world religions began to be reexamined. Inspired by people like the Methodist layman and Nobel Peace Prize winner John R. Mott, the modern ecumenical movement gained momentum among Protestants. Mott emphasized unity for the sake of mission and urged interreligious dialogue, not diatribe, as he pressed for world peace.[2]

From the 1960s forward, there has been an unprecedented degree of activity bent on enhancing religious understanding, cooperation, and unity. Roman Catholic ecumenical activity has been centered in the Vatican's Secretariat for Promoting Christian Unity, while the 345 member churches of the World Council of Churches represent roughly 500 million Protestant and Orthodox Christians in 110 countries. Perhaps due to the ecumenical DNA of Methodists, three of the seven general secretaries of the World Council of Churches since its inception in 1948 have been Methodist: Philip A. Potter of the West Indies (1972–84), Emilio Castro of Uruguay (1985–92), and Samuel Kobia of Kenya (2004–2009).

In recent years new efforts have been made to include Christians who belong to evangelical or charismatic churches and congregations in the ecumenical conversations. There have been two global gatherings (Nairobi, Kenya, 2007, and Manado, Indonesia, 2011) and the journey continues in order to broaden and deepen encounters on the way to Christian unity. United Methodists are involved and serve as bridge builders. At the recent global gathering in 2011, Bishop Joaquina Nhanala of Mozambique represented the Council of Bishops.

A recent survey revealed that around the world, United Methodists are engaged in grassroots efforts to promote Christian unity and interreligious relationships. Bishop Christian Alsted of the Nordic-Baltic Area describes United Methodists everywhere as being "bridge-builders, always connecting the gap between Catholics, Orthodox, Baptists, and Pentecostals." Bishop Rodolfo A. Juan of the Philippines describes his pastors as being "inclined to ecumenism" and "very open and friendly" to persons of different religious traditions. Bishop Nkula Ntanda Ntambo of the North Katanga Area of the Congo reports, "We work hand in hand with Catholic, Muslim, Pentecostal and indigenous religions. We respect one another and share prayer meetings, encourage dialogue, and in time of war work together for peace."[3]

FOUR KEY DIMENSIONS OF CHRISTIAN MISSION

United Methodists have identified four key dimensions of Christian mission that focus on making disciples of Jesus Christ for the transformation of the world. They are integral to the gospel expressions of our Methodist missional DNA and are shared in differing ways by other Christian communions of faith. Effective implementation of these ministries is enabled as we embrace attitudes and actions reflecting a quest for Christian unity and interreligious relationships.

United Methodists are focused on leadership development, congregational vitality, ministry with the poor, and global health. All are interrelated; none has priority over another. *First, our vision and mission is a commitment to develop principled Christian leaders for the church and world.* Around the world the church has emphasized loving God with one's mind and educating persons to meet their God-given potential. Ensuring a clergy and laity that are equipped with biblical and theological knowledge, who live lives of ethical integrity and intentionality, and who are oriented outward toward the world are basic to our understanding of the church.

Illustrative of our commitment has been the establishment around the world of schools, colleges, universities, and theological seminaries that have educated, not only United Methodists, but Christians of many persuasions, as well as persons of other faiths. Fostering understanding, engagement, and respect of persons with differing religious traditions always has been a hallmark of Methodism.

This commitment is further demonstrated by the response of United Methodist laity and clergy whenever disaster strikes anywhere in the world. Coordinated by the United Methodist Committee on Relief, we respond generously, not only with our money, but also with tireless volunteers who come to help in every way they can. These acts of service are often done in collaboration with ecumenical and interreligious partners. Working together in these ways the leaders that have been nurtured in our congregations demonstrate God's goodness to everyone.

Second, we believe in creating new places for new people by starting new congregations and revitalizing existing ones. Churches always are tempted to live off the spiritual endowment of the past rather than investing anew in making disciples for Jesus Christ. Declining church memberships too often reflect a failure to witness to our faith effectively and to strategically reach out to new, younger, and more diverse people in our neighborhoods and communities.

Around the globe United Methodists reach out to those yearning for a spiritual home. We aim to make disciples of Jesus Christ for the transformation of the world in a cooperative, not competitive, approach with other Christians. We celebrate our historic ties and contemporary relationships with others who share a Wesleyan heritage through participation in the World Methodist Council. We participate and promote ecumenical partnerships through local, national, regional, and world councils of churches.

We are both evangelical and ecumenical, as we underscore Jesus' command to "go therefore and make disciples of all nations, baptizing them in the name of the Father and of the Son and of the Holy Spirit, and teaching them to obey everything that I have commanded you" (Matthew 28:19-20 NRSV). Known often as the Great Commission, this biblical passage has helped inspire generations of Christians to share their faith in winsome and hospitable ways by creating congregations for spiritual sojourners

Engaging in ministry with the poor is a third focus imperative to our denomination. From its inception, the Wesleyan movement has taken literally the words of Jesus to feed the hungry, give drink to the thirsty, welcome the stranger, clothe the naked, care for the sick, clothe the naked, and visit the imprisoned (Matthew 25:31-45 NRSV). Just as we embrace the Great Commission, we also confirm the Great Commandment: "You shall love the Lord your God with all your heart, and with all your soul, and with all your mind" and "You shall love your neighbor as yourself" (Matthew 22:37-40 NRSV).

Our emphasis is that our ministry is *with* the poor, not just *to* the poor. We are companions and partners, learning and sharing with each other. This ministry is not a matter of charity, but of justice, as we stand in solidarity with those impoverished, stigmatized, and marginalized. We urge not simply random acts of kindness but systematic and strategic efforts aimed at alleviating and eliminating poverty, hunger, and disease. As television journalist and former Baptist pastor Bill Moyers observes:

> Charity is commendable; everyone should be charitable. But justice aims to create a social order in which, if individuals choose not to be charitable, people still don't go hungry, unschooled or sick without care. Charity depends on the vicissitudes of whim and personal wealth; justice depends on commitment instead of circumstance. Faith-based charity provides crumbs from the table; faith-based justice offers a place at the table.[4]

The movement initiated by John Wesley was characterized by a deep commitment to the poor. Wesley even saw ministry with the poor as a means of grace. Engaging with people at the margins brings us closer to where Jesus already is! At times, however, we get trapped in affluence and the status quo; we need to be challenged to move out of our comfort zones. Engaging in ministry with the poor in our communities and countries as well as other parts of the world deepens our understanding of the gospel and expands our bonds with brothers and sisters of other classes and cultures.

Closely related is the fourth focus: combating the diseases of poverty by improving health globally. Nowhere is our commitment to ecumenical and interreligious relationships more evident than in the United Methodist emphasis on combating diseases of poverty. Disease knows neither denomination nor religious persuasion. It is an equal-opportunity killer, particularly of the impoverished and especially women and children.

The church's global health initiative aims to raise awareness among our people; spark cooperation and partnership of church, secular society, and other religious groups; advocate enhanced public health policies; and mobilize financial support to stamp out diseases like malaria, AIDS, tuberculosis, and diarrhea-related illnesses.

Hoping to "walk the talk," United Methodists in recent years have raised almost $75 million in a campaign called "Imagine No Malaria." It has established fourteen health boards in Africa and Haiti where local church people distribute these funds to people who need it the most. They work in collaboration with other health professionals, government officials, and nongovernment organizations in ways that ensure transparency and accountability.

Additionally, the church through its mission agencies such as United Methodist Committee on Relief (UMCOR) has distributed millions of dollars to address health issues, attentive only to a person's need, not a person's creed. Combating stigma and discrimination, the United Methodist Global AIDS Fund has worked through local congregations and church agencies to fund HIV and AIDS ministries in thirty-seven countries. The General Board of Global Ministries and United Methodist Women fund global health programs around the world.

EBOLA CRISIS

Epitomizing the new way of living envisioned by the church's emphasis on Christian unity and interreligious relationships has been how United Methodist clergy and laity have responded to the pandemic of Ebola in West Africa. In this crisis, all four foci are manifest—principled leadership, renewed congregations, working with the poor, and addressing a disease of poverty.

This theological commitment to a new way of living becomes manifest in practical, life-saving ways. When the Ebola pandemic emerged with devastating consequences in western Africa, United Methodist laity and clergy courageously and compassionately responded to quell public fears and promote public health. Many died from the disease, often as a result of self-sacrificial caring for others. United Methodist Bishop John K. Yambasu of Sierra Leone led an organized ecumenical and interfaith effort. As chair of the Religious Leaders Task Force on Ebola, he declared:

> Ebola does not discriminate between Muslims and Christians. It does not discriminate between political parties. When it strikes, it kills anybody of any faith or political group. Now is the time that we must stand firm together as a nation to fight the Ebola scourge if we must survive as a nation.[5]

In neighboring Liberia, United Methodist Bishop John Innis texted members not to be misled by those denying the reality of the disease and who blamed health workers for its spread. Innis wrote: "Ebola is real. It kills with little warning. Please adhere to health messages to safeguard your family. Let us be in prayer. God is with us."[6]

By overcoming temptations to schism and religious rivalries as they pursued the public good, our African sisters and brothers have demonstrated anew what it means to "deepen and expand the ecumenical and interreligious ministries of The United Methodist Church."[7] They also underscore afresh the healing ministry of Jesus who prayed:

I ask not only on behalf of these, but also on behalf of those who will believe in me through their word, that they may all be one. As you, Father, are in me and I am in you, may they also be in us, so that the world may believe that you have sent me. (John 17:20-21 NRSV)

QUESTIONS

1. Why is Christian unity considered a gift from God, something to be maintained, not created?

2. Why is maintaining Christian unity and interreligious relationships not an option for United Methodists?

3. How do the four foci emphasized by United Methodists contribute to creating vital congregations that are seeking to transform the world?

4. In what ways are you and your church involved in fostering Christian unity and interreligious relationships? What else could be done?

NOTES

1. *The Book of Discipline of The United Methodist Church* (Nashville: The United Methodist Publishing House, 2012), ¶437, p. 348.

2. Benjamin L. Hartley, "'That They All Might Be One': John R. Mott's Contributions to Methodism, Interreligious Dialogue, and Racial Reconciliation," *Methodist Review: A Journal of Wesleyan and Methodist Studies*, Volume 4, 2012.

3. Cited in Donald E. Messer, "United Methodists Bridging Global Religious Divide," February 12, 2014, United Methodist News Service. http://umcconnections.org/2014/02/12/survey-united-methodists -bridging-global-religious-divide/.

4. Bill Moyers, forward to Jim Wallis, *Faith Works: How Faith-Based Organizations Are Changing Lives, Neighborhoods, and America* (New York: Random House, 2000).

5. Bishop John K. Yambasu quoted by Phileas Jusu, "Sierra Leone Task Force Targets Ebola," United Methodist News Service, July 28, 2014. http://www.umc.org/news-and-media/sierra-leone-task-force-targets-ebola.

6. Bishop John Innis quoted in "United Methodist Communications Fights Ebola with Technology," August 19, 2014. http://www.umc.org/news-and-media/united-methodist-communications-fights-ebola-with -technology.

7. *Book of Discipline*, ¶437.

In essentials, unity; in non-essentials, liberty; and, in all things, charity.

Rupertus Meldenius

Be tolerant with each other and, if someone has a complaint against anyone, forgive each other. As the Lord forgave you, so also forgive each other. And over all these things put on love, which is the perfect bond of unity.

Colossians 3:13-14

CHAPTER 2

Embracing Ecumenical and Interreligious Relationships

Mary Ann Swenson and Stephen J. Sidorak, Jr.

When it comes to things ecumenical and even interreligious, *The Book of Discipline of The United Methodist Church* does not equivocate. United Methodist ecumenical commitment has legal standing as defined within the Constitution:

> As part of the church universal, The United Methodist Church believes that the Lord of the church is calling Christians everywhere to strive toward unity; and therefore it will seek, and work for, unity at all levels of church life.[1]

This means ecumenism is not a denominational option, but an ecclesiological imperative for the "People Called Methodist."[2] *The Book of Discipline* in various sections outlines and underscores the range of United Methodist ecumenical and interreligious commitment, describing in some detail the many-sided nature of our commitment and offering a heartfelt affirmation of our calling to be "neighbors and witnesses to all peoples."[3]

In 2016 *The Book of Discipline* will add the word *pray* to the "Ecumenical Relations" section of the Constitution (¶6, Article VI), which is not just a symbolic gesture but a matter of substantive, spiritual significance.[4] When this happens, The United Methodist Constitution will clearly declare we are to "pray, seek, and work for, unity at all levels of church life." Disciplinary mandates are incumbent on all United Methodists and the means by which we show a demonstrable capacity to embrace both ecumenical and interreligious relationships.

In fact, our abiding commitment to the ecumenical movement is built on a constitutional confession. "The church of Jesus Christ exists in and for the world, and its very dividedness is a hindrance to its mission in that world."[5] The United Methodist Church acknowledges that disunity among Christians is scandalous, contrary to Christ's will for the disciples and a stumbling block before the world (see John 17:21). Our denominational commitment to ecumenical endeavor is irrevocable, because it is scripturally based.

John Wesley called us to live out of a "catholic spirit."[6] He declared, "If your heart is as my heart, give me your hand."[7] Critical to ecumenical mission today, this catholic or universal spirit must be recaptured in all of its poignant simplicity, theological sophistication, practical application, and, yes, interreligious relevance. Wesley's "catholic spirit" provides us a glimpse of the givenness of our togetherness in Christ Jesus. His sermon on the "catholic spirit" is a truly classic statement on the ecumenical predisposition, almost certainly a precious gift of prevenient grace.

RACISM AND UNITED METHODISM

Before further delineation of the ecumenical and interreligious commitment of The United Methodist Church can properly occur, attention must be paid to the reality of racism endemic in the

Methodist tradition. The church's Constitution declares "The United Methodist Church recognizes the sin of racism has been destructive to its unity throughout its history. Racism continues to cause painful division and marginalization."[8]

Ours is a church that looks first at its own house and confesses its dividedness, historically and currently. Consequently, our church "commits itself to strive toward closer relationship with other Methodist or Wesleyan churches wherever they may be found."[9] United Methodist concern for Christian unity begins with the tragic brokenness within the Methodist family. A critical element in the quest for Christian unity by The United Methodist Church has been, therefore, the restoration of unity among members of the Methodist family.

An ignominious history of blatant racism led to the breakup of Methodism into multiple denominations. The ongoing fragmentation of Methodism along racial lines undermines the unity of these churches, severely tests our commitment to "connectionalism," reawakens extremely painful memories, and continues to separate us one from the other. The "color line" that has been drawn has long been a blot on our denominational conscience.

It is theologically inexcusable and morally unconscionable that the other Pan-Methodist denominations came into being mainly due to racial barriers erected by the predecessor bodies of our own church. Lamentably, Methodism suffers from the self-inflicted wound of racism—in all its insidious manifestations. Yet, there has been proven dedication within The United Methodist Church to preserve a special relationship with the historic African-American Methodist churches that has been expressed through the Pan-Methodist Commission. The Pan-Methodist Commission exists in part to be a repairer of the breach. The unwavering will to overcome this relational rupture is courageous testimony to the sincere yearning for racial reconciliation.

The United Methodist Church institutionally and liturgically repented of its sin of racism and officially conducted acts of repentance at the 2000 and 2004 General Conferences, "for those who left" and "those who stayed behind," respectively. Members of the predominantly African-American Pan-Methodist churches and African-American members of The United Methodist Church have graciously forgiven "seventy times seven." Our church ought to be forever grateful for this undeserved forgiveness and be indefatigable in ongoing efforts to set our still segregated house in order, lest grace be cheap.

The persistence of racism and its "church-dividing" nature and the pernicious effects of "white privilege" continue to pose a threat to Methodist unity. It is incumbent on us to remain mindful of the intimate, familial factors inherent in the legacy of denominational racism. We trust United Methodist angst and anguish over racism offers testimony to other Wesleyans, as well as our other ecumenical partners, how seriously we take the racial divisions in Methodism and our determination to eliminate racism in our midst.

"O Happy Day" it was on May Day 2012 at the General Conference in Tampa, Florida, when the six churches of the Pan-Methodist Commission finally entered into a new, formal relationship of full communion with one another! Now, with full communion, there is a distinct possibility that new life for the Pan-Methodist Commission itself might obtain. Recently the Consultation of Methodist Bishops decided to meet every other year, rather than every four years, yet another sign of the potential for revitalization. We are sanguine about the prospects for the Pan-Methodist Commission. Becoming full communion partners with all the other member churches of the Pan-Methodist Commission is evidence of one more step taken toward the healing of relationships.

Let us embrace and celebrate the new full communion agreement with the African Methodist Episcopal Church, the African Methodist Episcopal Zion Church, the Christian Methodist Episcopal Church, the African Union Methodist Protestant Church, and the Union American Methodist Episcopal Church. Thanks be to God. And, let us hasten to note parenthetically, that ridding the body of Christ of the sin of racism is atop the agenda of a number of conciliar bodies.

We Have Need of One Another

Embedded in John Wesley's concept of "catholic spirit" is his realization that "a necessary consequence of [Christian] unity, [is] that the several members need one another."[10] Wesley is himself an example of persistent resistance to the perpetual temptation of many Christians who dare to say of other sisters and brothers in Christ, "I have no need of you" (cf. 1 Corinthians 12). Just the opposite, let us be hospitable to those parts of the body of Christ with whom we are in relationships, likewise with those with whom we have not yet entered into relationships. Let us consistently welcome where the Holy Spirit may be leading us, as we enter into new relationships in emerging forms of ecumenical life. Let us continually ask ourselves as Christians, "Do we strive to evince an ever-expansive responsiveness to the ecumenical vision and follow the promptings of the Holy Spirit in regard to relationships?"

The ecumenically astute statement known as the Lund Principle haunts us denominationally. The Lund Principle, articulated at the Third World Conference on Faith and Order held in Lund, Sweden, can be abbreviated to read:

> We would . . . earnestly request our Churches to consider whether they are doing all they ought to do to manifest the oneness of the people of God [and] ask themselves whether they are showing sufficient eagerness to enter into conversation with other Churches, and whether they should not act together in all matters except those in which deep differences of conviction compel them to act separately[.][11]

Threatening as this ecumenical principle can be denominationally and horrifying as it is institutionally, the Lund Principle nevertheless serves as indispensable and pragmatic wisdom, readily available to those who would take seriously the ecumenical commitment of The United Methodist Church.

Institutionally, The United Methodist Church has created a denominational office within the Council of Bishops that focuses especially on issues of Christian unity and interreligious relationships. Through this Office of Christian Unity and Interreligious Relationships, tough and probing questions are posed by the Lund Principle. These queries could embolden the Council of Bishops to call for *increased* connectional and ecumenical accountability among and between the general agencies of our church resulting in *greater* interagency ecumenical synergy across the connection—and beyond it. It could encourage each annual conference to take stock of the internal and external alignment of its own instrumentalities with the Lund Principle. Is there any correspondence between its own organizational *modus operandi* and the claims the Lund Principle makes on an annual conference to critique its inveterate tendencies to go it alone denominationally instead of searching unceasingly for ways to "act together in all matters" ecumenically? Does an annual conference reject out of hand the interrogation of itself the Lund Principle would conduct, or view its line of hard questioning as a genuine learning opportunity granted to it? Can an annual conference honestly testify that it is acting together in good faith with "all in each place" insofar as the Lund Principle is concerned? Implementation of the Lund Principle requires an ecumenical rebuke of the isolationism typical of denominationalism. Might it not mean we finally do the right things for the wrong reasons because we can no longer afford to do things separately? What once perhaps could be accomplished alone denominationally can barely be imagined any more ecumenically.

Being the largest of the ecumenically minded "mainline churches" in the United States and a worldwide communion, The United Methodist Church should inquire what else it could do in ecumenical *and* interreligious witness and service. Jesus said: "From everyone to whom much has been given, much will be required; and from the one to whom much has been entrusted, even more will be demanded" (Luke 12:48 NRSV). With the memory of these words of

Jesus reverberating in our ears, we trust the Office of Christian Unity and Interreligious Relationships will attain profound, fresh insight into its own structural importance within the Council of Bishops, since they have been assigned the collective responsibility "to lead the Church in its ecumenical and interreligious ministries."[12]

A Passion for the Unity of the Church

A bishop is described in *The Book of Discipline* as one who has "a passion for the unity of the church."[13] Would not a similar passion apply to all United Methodists? Is this not our calling as Christians, whether we are a layperson active in the world, a local pastor faithfully serving a parish, or a denominational leader entrusted to work through the Office of Christian Unity and Interreligious Relationships? Our common purpose is to deepen and expand, enhance and strengthen ecumenical and interreligious relationships. Would not both the church and world benefit from an unbound passion for things ecumenical and interreligious?

Theologically, United Methodists believe that "we see the Holy Spirit at work in making the unity among us more visible."[14] Anyone with eyes to see would say the same today. There is a growing awareness of the truth that our primary membership in a denomination is secondary to our relatedness in Christ Jesus.[15] Ultimately, what we *do* together as Christians is extremely important, but who we *are* together is absolutely paramount.

A New Leaf in the Ecumenical Table

Today, a "catholic spirit" would necessarily include an inter-religious dimension. Interreligious hospitality is the new leaf that has been inserted into the ecumenical table. Our participation in conciliar work and the nurturing of ecumenical relationships can be outstripped only by our earnest dedication to ensure the Christian community is ecumenically engaged interreligiously.

We are on record as a denomination that prefers the risk of vigorous encounter with "other living faiths" to the escape of insipid interreligious separatism. The United Methodist Council of Bishops has clearly recognized that "to take risks for the gospel and to converse with different cultures and living faiths are, indeed, ecumenical tasks under the lordship of Christ." Further, they have professed that "the interreligious activities of The United Methodist Church are responses to God's presence in all cultures and religions. These reasonable acts in no way diminish commitment to the lordship of Christ."[16]

The Christian foundation for interreligious relationships derives from the root meaning of the word *religion,* which is to be "bound together." The notion that to be religious means to be bound together can have salutary influence on the planetary future. We can become informed on the deeper meaning of what it means to be religious— to be bound together—even under duress. In interreligious relationships, we can discover how "to bind up" (another root meaning of the word *religion*) the wounds that have hurt us historically and plague us currently.

In-depth interreligious exchange with each other about all that we share in heart and mind and attentive listening to one another about all that continues to divide us is a solemn duty. With the Yale theologian William Sloane Coffin, Jr., we can remind ourselves that the remarkable thing is not so much that so many individuals believe different things. It is that so many different individuals devoutly hold so much in common. Nowadays, we have discerned a new pertinence[17] to the apostle Paul's wise counsel in 1 Corinthians 12. Just as no Christian can dare say to another, "I have no need of you," Christians cannot feel free to behave as if they have "no need of" Jews or Muslims—"no need of" those of any religious tradition different from their own. We realize in entirely new ways how Christians are interrelated with "all life" interreligiously in what Dr. Martin Luther King, Jr., termed "an inescapable network of mutuality, tied in a single garment of destiny."[18]

We believe in a truly ecumenical church in a wonderfully interreligious world. Immersion in interreligious life can make us better United Methodists and stronger Christians. May we instill in United Methodists what the Swedish bishop and New Testament scholar, Krister Stendahl, called "holy envy"—the mutual respect, complete affection, and sacred trust those of one religious tradition can feel for those of a different one.[19] May that "holy envy" be perfected!

IN CONCLUSION

We have only begun to adumbrate how and why The United Methodist Church embraces unreservedly ecumenical and interreligious relationships. We know that many, including too many United Methodists, altogether ignore these kinds of relationships or often neglect to tend to them solicitously. Our hope for the ecumenical future is that all would embrace and celebrate the richness of the oneness we Christians enjoy in Christ Jesus our Lord.

We also hope we would embrace the oneness of the witness for peace and justice, for *shalom,* that God would have us bear to the world with sundry sisters and brothers of a variety of different religious traditions and all people of good will, religiously affiliated or not. The *oikoumene,* the whole inhabited earth, cries out for such concerted witness. Pierre Teilhard de Chardin once said: "The future belongs to those who give the next generation reason for hope." We believe those who openly and enthusiastically embrace ecumenical and interreligious relationships will be found in that kind of company.

Let it be so, we pray.

QUESTIONS

1. Why is asking United Methodists to "pray" for "unity at all levels of church life" more than a symbolic gesture?

2. What is meant by the "catholic spirit" enunciated by John Wesley, and why it is important to United Methodists today?

3. How can United Methodists at a congregational level address racism and contribute to reconciliation in our church and society?

4. In what way is the Lund Principle relevant in our relations with other churches in the community?

5. What can we do to enhance interreligious relationships?

NOTES

1. *The Book of Discipline of The United Methodist Church* (Nashville: The United Methodist Publishing House, 2012), The Constitution, ¶6, Article VI, p. 25.

2. Ibid., "Ecumenical Commitment," ¶105, p. 88.

3. Ibid.

4. This was approved through the current quadrennial constitutional amendment process.

5. *The Book of Discipline*, The Constitution, "Preamble," p. 23.

6. Ibid., ¶103, "Our Doctrinal History," p. 54.

7. John Wesley, Sermon 39, "A Catholic Spirit"; http://www.crivoice.org /cathspirit.html.

8. *The Book of Discipline*, ¶5, Article V, p. 24.

9. Ibid., ¶433.3, p. 346.

10. Wesley's Notes on the Bible, http://biblehub.com/commentaries /wes/1_corinthians/12.htm.

11. Lund Principle, Third World Conference on Faith and Order held in Lund, Sweden in 1952. http://www.gccuic-umc.org/index .php?option=com_content&task=view&id=260&Itemid=196.

12. *The Book of Discipline*, ¶436, p. 347; see also ¶¶431-42, pp. 342-49.

13. Ibid., ¶403.e, p. 317.

14. Ibid., ¶105, "Ecumenical Commitment," p. 88.

15. Ibid.

16. United Methodist Council of Bishops, March 30, 1978, statement, "Christian Unity: Imperatives and New Commitments."

17. See *The Book of Discipline*, ¶105, "Ecumenical Commitment," p. 88.

18. Martin Luther King, Jr., *Letter from a Birmingham Jail*, 16 April 1963.

19. Douglas Martin, "Krister Stendahl, 86, Ecumenical Bishop, Is Dead," *New York Times*, April 16, 2008; http://www.nytimes.com/2008/04/16 /us/16stendahl.html?_r=0.

That there might be no schism in the body. (1 Corinthians 12:25)
Schism "is evil in itself. To separate ourselves from a body of living Christians, with whom we were before united, is a grievous breach of the law of love. It is the nature of love to unite us together; and the greater the love, the stricter the union. And while this continues in its strength, nothing can divide those whom love has united. It is only when our love grows cold, that we can think of separating from our brethren. And this is certainly the case with any who willingly separate from their Christian brethren. The pretenses for separation may be innumerable, but want of love is always the real cause; otherwise they would still hold the unity of the Spirit in the bond of peace."

John Wesley, Sermon 75

Now I encourage you, brothers and sisters, in the name of our Lord Jesus Christ: Agree with each other and don't be divided into rival groups. Instead, be restored with the same mind and the same purpose. My brothers and sisters, Chloe's people gave me some information about you, that you're fighting with each other.

1 Corinthians 1:10-11

CHAPTER 3

REMEMBERING OUR ECUMENICAL HERITAGE

GLEN ALTON MESSER II
AND BENJAMIN L. HARTLEY

The Christian faith makes the bold claim that God incarnated in Jesus of Nazareth and entered into human history. Not all religions make historical claims that stake out specific locations on the timeline of lived experience. It is an aspect of who we are as Christians that we mark our relationship with the Creator in a way that both transcends the confines of time (*kairos*) and brings it close to us through an inherent involvement in our days, years, and eras (*chronos*).[1] The relationship between the Christian life and history is underscored by our sacred liturgies that rehearse for us— and involve us—in the story of faith. We recall the life, death, and resurrection of Jesus.[2] We recall the communion of saints of which all Christians of the past, present, and future are gathered together in the eternal presence of God (Hebrews 11). To keep an eye toward the historical is, in a very real way, to keep one oriented toward the most essential elements of the living faith of those who walk along the Way with Christ Jesus.

Remembering the Necessity of Unity

History is, likewise, an essential tool and practice for those whose life and ministry includes calling Christians to remember the necessity of unity. History is, in itself, a pursuit that unifies those called by Christ Jesus. History gives us perspective to see beyond one moment in time toward a more encompassing view of the work of God and God's creatures. History helps us think and act with an honesty of motivation that frees us from being driven away from our mark by currents and winds of fears, passions, and tumults. History is a tool—a discipline of both the heart and the mind—that is integral to the pursuit of Christian unity in the Christian life.

As a discipline of both the heart and the mind, however, it is important to stress that history can be used poorly and even wrongly. It is a discipline that requires seriousness of consideration, and sometimes our discipline in history—as in Christian devotion—is less faithful than it ought to be. A simplistic "proof texting" of historical events that shuts down conversation instead of promoting it must be firmly rejected. It is also not right to say—as some do—that all perspectives are valid. Some data are unreliable. Much data upon which historical interpretations rely is missing (never having been retained or discovered). And the overlay of biases (conscious and unconscious) can taint the reliability and appropriateness of a historical portrayal. By necessity, all histories should be, and remain, open to review, to testing, to revision, and, if necessary, to partial or full refutation.

For United Methodists the right use of and growth in historical understanding may sound somewhat analogous to the Spirit-led growth in personal and social holiness that has been the animating lifeblood for the Methodist movement for generations. John Wesley's *Plain Account of Christian Perfection* illustrates this spirit of correction and growth in holiness:

> "Love is the fulfilling of the law, the end of the commandment." It is not only "the first and great" command, but all the commandments in one. "Whatsoever things are just, whatsoever things are pure, if

there be any virtue, if there be any praise," they are all comprised in this one word, love. In this is perfection, and glory, and happiness: The royal law of heaven and earth is this, "Thou shall love the Lord thy God with all thy heart, and with all thy soul, and with all thy mind, and with all thy strength." The one perfect good shall be your one ultimate end. One thing shall ye desire for its own sake, – the fruition of Him who is all in all. One happiness shall ye propose to your souls, even an union with Him that made them, the having "fellowship with the Father and the Son," the being "joined to the Lord in one spirit." One design ye are to pursue to the end of time, – the enjoyment of God in time and in eternity. Desire other things so far as they tend to this; love the creature, as it leads to the Creator. But in every step you take, be this the glorious point that terminates your view. Let every affection, and thought, and word, and action, be subordinate to this. Whatever ye desire or fear, whatever ye seek or shun, whatever ye think[,] speak, or do, be it in order to your happiness in God, the sole end, as well as source, of your being.[3]

The Methodist movement was based on telling stories of growth and development (and "backsliding") as people sought to learn from one another's testimony and the testimony of the Holy Spirit in their efforts to grow more perfect in love. Recording the history of the Methodist movement for Wesley was not only to "get the facts right" but was a way to learn from experience that the movement might continue to grow in its pursuit of holiness corporately and as individuals. History was filled with God's dynamism.

John Wesley and Christian Unity

John Wesley's own work as a historian of the Methodist movement, and as author of the four-volume *Concise History of England*, illustrates that he viewed history in a more dynamic way than many modern Westerners do today. Allan Nevins describes history as a kind of "bridge connecting the past and the present, and pointing the road to the future."[4] We believe Wesley would have resonated with this idea. But sometimes his "bridge" confused things as much as it clarified them. Wesley's own assessment of the history of Britain, for example, reflected a sense of inevitability of ever-increasing liberty— even if he also condemned those whom he believed took liberty too far. Historians today rightly point out that Wesley's view of history as an inevitable march toward increasing liberty was a serious flaw in his work as a historian even though it also illustrates his hopefulness concerning human potential.[5]

Similarly, it is important to identify the missteps of Wesley as well as his triumphs with regard to the work of Christian unity. In recent decades it has become commonplace to make reference to Wesley's sermon "A Catholic Spirit" when one wishes to empha- size how ecumenical the Wesleyan movement has been in the past. Indeed, Wesley's words are inspiring: "'If thine heart is as my heart,' if thou lovest God and all mankind, I ask no more: 'give me thine hand.'"[6] The Methodist historian who is engaged in ecumenical efforts must also be mindful, however, of Wesley's less than charita- ble remarks toward, for example, Roman Catholics, as well as other groups.[7] In the late nineteenth century it is sadly not difficult to find virulently anti-Catholic remarks as well among Methodist leaders.[8]

We do not make reference to these stories to give ourselves a browbeating by airing the dirty laundry of our past; there is an important lesson here for persons engaged in ecumenism. It is not necessarily the case that more dialogue—regardless of its quality— will always and everywhere result in "progress" toward ever increas- ing levels of Christian unity. Sometimes ecumenical work takes steps backward. It is the task of historians and theologians who know who they are as Methodists and Christians to discern when that may be happening and to make "course corrections" as needed.

ECUMENICAL MINISTRY AS BRIDGE-MAKING

The notion that history is a bridge that we discussed above is an important concept in understanding the place of history in the Christian faith and in the pursuit of Christian unity. Like the minister who calls the people's attention to the story of faith in the recitation of the eucharistic prayer, the historian calls people's attention to their relationship with the past, the present, and the future. Historians practice what the Rev. Dr. Robert Williams calls the "ministry of memory."[9] They remember—by drawing together the scattered bits of what was with the scattered bits of what is—and they offer up interpretations that help people make meaning of the vast scope of time and human experience. They help people examine what has happened, what is happening, and what may happen, so that they may use their free will to live faithfully and responsibly in the present moment.

Christian unity, the assertion that the church is one, is a recognition that even in its diversity the church is interconnected, integrally related in its particularities. Ecumenical ministry is another kind of bridge-making. Its efforts are rooted in calling to mind the kinship of all Christians (in that we are all called to God in and through Christ Jesus). Its efforts also point to the present moment and offer up meanings that point out the unity (or lack of unity) of Christians now. And its efforts point the way to the road forward toward a more dynamic embodiment of Christ's love in and among Christians throughout God's creation.

These ministries of ecumenism and history are in important conversation with each other. They help keep each other honest in our tasks and in our achievements. The pursuit of faithful embodiment of Christian unity challenges historical interpretations to keep an eye toward the mission of Christ Jesus as something pursued on behalf of all creation. Do our histories make the stories of some too grand and diminish the stories of others? Who of God's children are ignored? What of God's sacred creativity is spoken about and what is not? Histories cannot, in practical terms, include everything and everyone. But do they point to an honest portrayal of what has been included and what has been left out? Similarly, history challenges ecumenism not to overly simplify the story of Christian unity. It can ask many of the same questions that ecumenism can ask of the works of history. It can champion the forgotten, the excluded, and the oppressed.

RESTORING "A CHURCH DIVIDED"

If we apply the same need to test the claims of history to testing the claims of ecumenical endeavors, one place we might begin is to ask what we mean by "a church divided." Much has been written during the era of twentieth-century conciliar ecumenism about restoring the divided church and making it whole again.

Indeed, Methodists in a number of different ways have been among the most important leaders of Protestant efforts in ecumenism. Methodist layman John R. Mott (1865–1955) has been described as one of the key "architects" for the World Council of Churches' establishment in 1948. His work as an evangelist and organizer of student groups in the decades preceding the establishment of the World Council of Churches is a testimony to the power of friendship as well as administrative acumen for the sake of ecumenism. Since 1948, three of the six general secretaries of the WCC have come from representatives of global Methodism: Philip A. Potter of Dominica in the Caribbean, Emilio Castro of Uruguay, and Samuel Kobia of Kenya all provided valuable leadership to the ecumenical movement in its efforts to heal church division and to "restore" lost Christian unity.[10]

The historian engaged in efforts to promote Christian unity, however, must question assumptions about "restoring" Christian unity that may not have been as unified even in the early church as we would like to think.[11] The ecumenical movement in recent decades has further understood Christian unity (especially among many in relation to Central and Western Europe) in terms of institutional unity—with "church" being understood as an institutional vessel of the Holy Spirit in the world.[12] However, was it ever true that some of the churches in Africa and Asia were institutionally bound to the Roman Catholic Church? Some of these churches are clearly as ancient as the Roman Catholic Church, but their histories have tended to be downplayed if not forgotten by the mainstream of ecumenical endeavors in recent decades.[13]

Unity and the Holy Spirit

The understanding of "unity" in an institutional formulation also stakes out a theological understanding of "church" that is at odds with other understandings of the workings of the Holy Spirit (not seen as contained in specific and necessary institutional vessels). Many Pentecostal, Charismatic Christian, and other churches have ways of thinking about "church" that defy broad-brush definitions. A particularly good case in point here is with African Initiated Churches today.[14] While many have said that appeals to these Pentecostal and charismatic understandings of *pneumatology*[15] are "church-dividing," the opposite argument can logically be made if the starting point for unity is understood to be Christ Jesus' call upon us rather than a unified, institutional church's ultimate claim to be Christ's shepherds on earth.

If one accepts—and some do and some do not—that all Christians were once institutionally unified in one church, "church-dividing" means any diversity in polity and doctrine that is exercised outside of that frame. But, if one concedes that there have always been Christians who have lived in different institutional realities outside of that one, unifying, institution, then history gives a reality-check to what we can logically call "division" in the body of Christ.

Questions to Ask of Ecumenism

This is an especially important example of the kinds of questions that history can ask of ecumenism. All of this is even more important as we prepare to mark the five-hundredth anniversary of the 1517 start of what has been called the "Protestant Reformation." To be sure, the hatred, animosity, and bloodshed that followed cannot be condoned when seen in light of the command of Christ Jesus to love one another as he first loved us. But what of the birth of Protestant churches? What of the birth of Christian communities that preceded this particular dating of different ways of being Christian in Europe?

(Jan Hus [1369–1415] and the Moravians come to mind, as do the Waldensians, who trace their "Protestant" origins to the late 1100s.) What of those whose origins as Christian churches come *after* the Reformation struggles (notably the Methodists)? Are we to see every one of these expressions of Christian faith as a mistake—or even a rebellion against God?

Or is there another way of looking at things? Instead of seeing the Christian church as a monolith that has broken into pieces that need to be gathered and reassembled, what if we instead use the metaphor of the living organism? If one looks at the life, ministry, death, and resurrection of Jesus—followed by Pentecost—as the beginning of the church in the world, the expansion of Christianity through new and contextualized forms (the cellular division and particularization of functions of Christian communities) could be understood as the growth—and not the fracturing—of the body of Christ. The unity of that body is Christ himself.

The harmonious relationship among Christians (defined by love among one another and bold expressions of love toward those whose lives are lived outside the church) is a mark of the integrity of the church. Here may well be an understanding that truly invites all Christians without demanding they crawl back into an ecclesial institution that remains a poor fit for their way of following Christ, which they hold dear.

These are practical examples of the questions one may faithfully and intelligently ask. These are core questions that history and ecumenism together can meditate upon in order to faithfully discern a way forward as we remember those who went before us and will come after us.

QUESTIONS

1. What difference does it make that Christianity makes historical claims about its founder and faith?

2. Why is it important to recognize that John Wesley did not always live up to the "catholic spirit" he professed?

3. In what ways could ecumenical ministry be "bridge-making" in our community or society?

4. In striving for Christian unity, are we seeking to "restore" a previous unity or reach a new level never before known?

5. In what ways is the church not a broken monolith but instead a living organism?

NOTES

1. The New Testament uses a few different terms to convey different meanings of time. *Kairos* refers to the fullness of God's time interacting in human history. The Incarnation, for example, is the ultimate *kairos* event. *Chronos*, by contrast, is a bit more mundane. It refers simply to the sequential passage of time and events in human history.

2. Indeed, early Christians used the theologically rich term *anamnesis* to express something even more profound than an intellectual recalling of previous events. The term *anamnesis* refers to a kind of mystical "making present" what has occurred before. Robert Louis Wilken is quite eloquent on this point in *The Spirit of Early Christian Thought: Seeking the Face of God* (New Haven: Yale University Press, 2003), pp. 33–34. See also "A Service of Word and Table 1" in *The United Methodist Hymnal* (Nashville: The United Methodist Publishing House, 1989), pp. 6–11. Apostles' and Nicene creeds are in *The United Methodist Hymnal*, 880, 881.

3. *The Works of John Wesley*, 3rd Edition, Volume 11: *Thoughts, Addresses, Prayers, and Letters*. (Grand Rapids: Baker Books, 2002), pp. 366–67.

4. Allan Nevins, *The Gateway to History*, Revised ed. (Garden City, NY: Anchor Books/Doubleday & Company, 1962), p. 14.

5. It is important to stress, however, that Wesley was no radical democrat. More modern phrases like "power to the people" would have prompted strong qualification by Wesley who still believed in the divine right of kings and strongly critiqued, for example, the American Revolution after he first supported it. William Gibson, "'The Past Is Another Country': Wesley's History of England," unpublished plenary presentation at the Oxford Institute for Methodist Theological Studies, Oxford, England, August 2013. We wish to thank Professor Gibson for kindly making available a manuscript copy of his 2013 address.

6. John Wesley, "Catholic Spirit: Sermon 39," http://wesley.nnu.edu/john-wesley/the-sermons-of-john-wesley-1872-edition/sermon-39-catholic-spirit/. Accessed on 4 March 2015.

7. On John Wesley's anti-Catholic attitudes, see David Butler, *Methodists and Papists: John Wesley and the Catholic Church in the Eighteenth Century* (London: Darton, Longman & Todd, 1995).

8. See, for example, Benjamin L. Hartley, *Evangelicals at a Crossroads: Revivalism and Social Reform in Boston, 1860-1910* (Durham: University of New Hampshire Press, 2011), pp. 65-92.

9. Robert Williams was General Secretary of the General Commission on Archives and History of The United Methodist Church from 2006 to 2014.

10. Paul Wesley Chilcote, "Evangelism in the Methodist Tradition," in *T & T Clark Companion to Methodism*, ed. Charles Yrigoyen, Jr. (New York: Bloomsbury T & T Clark, 2014), p. 231.

11. The title of Vatican II's Decree on Ecumenism is *Unitatis Redintegratio*, which translated means "restoration of unity." See Austin Flannery, OP, ed., *Vatican Council II: The Conciliar and Postconciliar Documents*, New Revised Edition 1992 (Northport, NY: Costello Publishing Company, 1992), p. 452.

12. For a solid example of how the history of ecumenism has generally portrayed the church and its development, please see Thomas E. Fitzgerald, *The Ecumenical Movement: An Introductory History* (Westport, CT: Praeger, 2004).

13. The Ethiopian Church can trace its history at least as far back as the early fourth century. The Acts of Thomas, which scholars estimate to be from around the year 200, has been described as the earliest account of the church far beyond the bounds of the Roman Empire (India). The early history of Persian Christianity is similarly rather unknown since, in seminary curricula, the early history of Christianity is largely limited to that which took place in the Roman Empire. On the early history of Christianity beyond the Roman Empire in Asia see Samuel Hugh Moffett, *A History of Christianity in Asia, Volume 1: Beginnings to 1500* (Maryknoll, NY: Orbis, 2006), 25.

14. Marthinus L. Daneel, *All Things Hold Together: Selected Essays by M. L. Daneel* (Pretoria, Republic of South Africa: University of South Africa Press, 2007), pp. 1-20.

15. Pneumatology is the study of the theology of the Holy Spirit.

To take risks for the gospel and to converse with different cultures and living faiths are, indeed, ecumenical tasks under the lordship of Christ. . . . The interreligious activities of The United Methodist Church are responses to God's presence in all cultures and religions. These reasonable acts in no way diminish commitment to the lordship of Christ.

United Methodist Council of Bishops
"Christian Unity: Imperatives and New Commitments,"
March 30, 1978

Christ is just like the human body—a body is a unit and has many parts, and all the parts of the body are one body, even though there are many. We were all baptized by one Spirit into one body, whether Jew or Greek, or slave or free, and we all were given one Spirit to drink.

1 Corinthians 12:12-13

CHAPTER 4

Identifying with Our Interreligious Traditions

Hee-Soo Jung

Christian unity is deeply embedded in the history of the Methodist movement, as evidenced in Wesley's "Catholic Spirit: Sermon 39," in which he affirmed:

> Though we cannot think alike, may we not love alike? May we not be of one heart, though we are not of one opinion? Without all doubt, we may. Herein all the children of God may unite, notwithstanding these smaller differences.[1]

It is my conviction that in our day, we need a similar openness to people of faith who are adherents of other approaches to the one God we worship in various ways.

Seeking Interfaith Relationships

Catholic theologian Hans Küng has written a guide for interreligious relationships contending that

> we need a dialogue with give and take, into which the deepest intentions of the religions must be introduced. Thus it must be a

critical dialogue, in which all religions are challenged not simply to justify everything, but to deliver their best and most profound message. In short we need a dialogue in mutual responsibility and in the awareness that none of us possesses the truth "ready–made," but are all in the way to the "ever greater" truth.[2]

Küng's precepts are a practical guide for churches' interfaith relationships today:

> There is no demanding the impossible of religions and the churches, it is merely asking them to live up to their own programs and basic intentions, asking them to direct their appeals for peace not only toward the outside, important as it is, but to the inside as well, and thus to do deeds of reconciliation and set up signs of peace in their own backyards. We can be sure that these deeds of reconciliation, that these signs of peace, will not fail to radiate powerful signals onto the fields of conflict "out there."[3]

God has blessed our churches with a kindred spirit of harmony and respect for global interfaith families. My strong belief is in the need for seeking interfaith relationships at all practical levels of our lives. God's creation has brought forth many faith traditions. The Christian community seeks visible forms of unity among neighbors. We move from an emphasis upon structural and institutional unity to one that finds its focus in relationships and mission centered in Jesus Christ.

We United Methodists are part of two great traditions: holiness and hospitality. Holiness urges us to live personal lives that follow the ethical path we believe that we have been bidden to live by Jesus (or by what we have come to believe "about" Jesus). Hospitality urges us to demonstrate radical welcoming and care of all, especially including those most different from our own selves.

In my pastoral attitude and witness I am eager to form life-giving relations of mutual respect. These relationships have gifted me in many blessed ways in my spiritual and academic journey. I engaged in academic graduate Buddhist studies in the late 1970s. I anticipated an open academic journey, but faced many conflicted emotions. I faced much turmoil in my inner life. I found out that my Christian-ness was sometimes rigid and dogmatic. It was a struggle for me to be at ease, even with the smells, postures, and colors of Buddhist temples. It was a gradual process of regaining comfort with the culture of my early upbringing. But eventually, being with Buddhist friends, shar-ing foods and fellowship have permeated me with wonder and sweet-ness of relationship. Slowly the sharp edge smoothed into sojourning together. It became easy for me to be a Christian among Buddhists, and they honored me as a Christian friend.

Different traditions and cultures are gifts to the global commu-nity when we are honest about inner feelings and proactively pro-cess together. We recognize each other in preciousness of giftedness. Conflict is God's gift to us because we need each other.

Living together with other religious traditions requires open-ness to change and being changed while we journey together. We need the dynamism and discernment that comes from speaking with others whose thinking differs from our own. We need those whose uniqueness and differences complement our own uniqueness and differences.

In my sermon at the 2008 General Conference, I spoke of ten-sions and conflicts as God's ongoing tests for humanity, demanding living together with love and dignity.

> One could argue that those who espouse greater openness are holding fast to biblical principles of hospitality. Those who desire clarity in matters of boundaries, however, are adhering to biblical principles of holiness. Both holiness and hospitality are excellent values. Both are biblical values, and both are right.

> Of course, they can also both be wrong. The problem is this: When we concern ourselves only with holiness, we become rigid and inward looking. We make an idol of our purity. When we concern ourselves only with hospitality, however, we lose our sense of who we are. We become so open to others that we lose the language of our own faith.[4]

In living with other religious traditions, I have come to appreciate the holiness and hospitality traditions honored in our daily practices even more. But I start to identify a kind of false pressure of Christian living, which is the temptation to dogmatically proclaim that one religion is true and the rest are false. Most of us have operative ideas about the diversity of religious traditions that fall somewhere along this spectrum between holiness and hospitality. Harvard professor Diana Eck grew up in the rural United Methodist churches of Montana, becoming a distinguished scholar of world religions. I am in deep agreement with Diana Eck when she writes:

> It is a question about the destiny of our human community and our capacity to listen with openness and empathy to people of faith very different from ourselves. It is a question about how we, whoever we are, understand the religious faith of others.[5]

A KOREAN PERSPECTIVE

Personal experience has shaped my faith and understanding. I was born on Kang-hwa, near the 38th parallel, the dividing line between the north and south of the Korean peninsula established at the end of WWII. This division of Korea was never endorsed by Koreans. It was imposed by the superpowers to advance their own agendas. For centuries the Korean peninsula had existed as a single people. The division into two nations occurred in 1945 after the Allied defeat of Japan, which had occupied Korea. Control, however, was not returned to Koreans, who for centuries had proven their leadership competency. The superpowers saw an opportunity to expand their world domination. The Soviets and the United States agreed to divide administration of the Korean peninsula, the Soviets taking over the North, the US taking over the South. Methodists were there and ready in the South, as Syngman Rhee, a Methodist, became its president in 1948.

The Korean conflict that occurred in the early 1950s had to do more with the conflict between the USSR and the USA than with any inherent differences between the Koreans of north and south. Koreans of north and south had never acted or desired to divide themselves. Koreans were divided by others for purposes having nothing to do with the welfare of Korea.

My most personally shattering encounter with the conflict between north and south occurred when I was swimming with a childhood friend. He found an interesting floating object. He reached out for it. A floating mine. An explosion. My friend was no more.

In my more mature years, these experiences of the division of Korea became the source of my growing awareness that so-called animosities between people often have to do not with the people but with the lust for power among the already powerful. Koreans of north and south were families with similar hopes and dreams. The USSR and the US had other ideas, so they made enemies of those who had for ages been a single people.

I was born into a family with a proud lineage. I was greatly honored when entrusted with the ancient records of our genealogy. Some thirteen years ago, an uncle of mine arrived in Green Bay. He had never traveled beyond the borders of Korea, but he came unannounced to entrust to me precious family records, reaching back many, many centuries. No honor could be greater in my culture. (Asian family heritage had been carefully kept for centuries before Western genealogy was preserved, so it goes farther back into our past.)

My birth family was Buddhist and Confucian. But at the age of sixteen, I was welcomed by the pastor of the Methodist church on Kang-hwa to become Christian. I gladly accepted the good news preached by Jesus of God's love for all, and I was accepted into that fledgling congregation.

As a new Christian and typical teenager, I was determined to reject my Buddhist and Confucian heritage. I began to see everything from my past, from Buddhism and Confucianism, as "bad" and everything Christian as "good." This became the source of some bad decisions that I made. The decision I most regret was my refusal to take part in the traditional burial rights for my father. Others trekked up the mountain for his burial. I refused to participate, saying, "This isn't Christian." Not until years later, well into my adult life, did I return to Kang-hwa and make that journey up the mountain to honor my father.

EXCLUSIVE VERSUS INCLUSIVE VIEWS

There is no other God than God—whatever name is used to speak of the Holy One. That's what I now have come to believe and understand. People of faith are exactly that, whatever their tradition. The differences between people of faith are far more pronounced *within* each tradition than *between* the traditions. Extremism exists in every faith tradition, extremists who believe that their way is "the only way." Within Christianity, we are familiar with the affirmation of the Johannine Jesus that "I am the way." Unfortunately, some of us have taken this cryptic comment about "The Way" and concluded that certain creedal affirmations about Jesus must be accepted, or hell is the alternative for those who might well be inclined not "to follow Jesus—his life and teachings."

At the center of virtually all faith groups are those who (1) live lives of gratitude for what they have been given, (2) live lives that acknowledge divine power greater than their own, and (3) believe they are called to live a life of gratitude and of respect of that power that is beyond their own. But there are also those who take their faith to an extreme that distorts their own faith.

On the conservative side, many are quite certain they have the correct understanding of exactly what their god expects/demands. On the other side are those who find no grounding in any faith tradition and are left wandering around in a search for elusive meaning. Somewhere between is the faith that Jesus of Nazareth lived and taught. And the faith of Jesus (not "about" Jesus) is closely akin to the core beliefs of most of the major faith traditions.

Within Christianity, there are those who insist on believing certain things "about" Jesus. Thus they become exclusive by nature, for, whatever they believe "about" Jesus, there are only a limited number who agree. But the wonderful option is to follow the faith "of" Jesus, to live in accord with the life he lived and taught. That faith accepts all humans as precious to God. That inclusive faith affirms that every one of us is a beloved child of God. That faith knows that this is the "gospel," the "good news" of God's love for us all. I have been moved by the writings of Diana L. Eck:

> I do not believe that our faith in Christ can lead us any longer along the road of intolerance and exclusivism. The road runs contrary to the spirit of Jesus of Nazareth. Faith in Christ means that I live my life, and will surely die my death, in terms of my commitment to Christ. It does *not* mean that no other experience of God's presence and mercy could possibly be true and serve to anchor someone else's life and transfigure someone else's death. It does *not* mean that I am somehow unfaithful if I also delight in the vision of playful, ecstatic, and tender love that Krishna reveals of God, for a visit to the community of Krishna in Brindavan brings all the pleasure of a visit to someone else's warm extended family. It does *not* mean that those Buddhists who do not use the word *God* at all but steadfastly cultivate stillness of mind toward the twin goals of wisdom and compassion are lost on the path.[6]

PRACTICAL STEPS TO ENHANCE INTERRELIGIOUS RELATIONSHIPS

As I reaffirm interreligious relations of United Methodists, I am reminded by E. Stanley Jones's invitation to friends from other faith traditions:

> Let everyone be perfectly free, for we are a family circle; we want each one to feel at home, and we will listen with reverence and respect to what each man has to share.[7]

In E. Stanley Jones's missionary journeys in India, he extended the spirit of hospitality to other faith leaders in the land. He saw his relationship and radical hospitality to other faiths as vital missional strategy. My own faith walk seeks to enlarge a family circle big enough to include other faiths.

When I was assigned as a bishop to the Wisconsin Area in 2012, I knew the disturbing news of the hate-motivated murderous assault on the Sikh Temple in South Milwaukee. But I found solace in the fact that our nearest United Methodist congregation immediately responded with compassion and hosted a community worship service to mourn the tragedy.

As United Methodists, we are called to bring God's vision of a different kind of world in which people of many faith traditions live together in peace. As United Methodists, we proclaim that God calls us to work together with all people to overcome injustice.

The United Methodist Book of Resolutions affirms that our Muslim neighbors are our coworkers in making "God's justice a reality for all people."[8] All people of faith have sacred traditions. The Qur'an embodies the tradition for our Muslim neighbors.

As United Methodists, we are clear in our faith—the faith of Jesus. We have experienced his transforming presence! Through and in Jesus we experience God's redeeming love and healing. In Jesus, we are renewed as God's creation. In Jesus, we have received an authentic life of salvation. Through Jesus, we have learned to say: "God is good!"

In my role as bishop, I have taken several steps to improve interfaith relationships. One step, while I was in Chicago, was to create a "Declaration of Relationship" with the Council of Islamic Organizations of Greater Chicago. I believe it can serve as a model for other Christians, so I have included the entire pledge here:

> We, members of the Council of Islamic Organizations of Greater Chicago and the Northern Illinois Conference of The United Methodist Church, believe it is imperative that people of faith commit

to a spirit of peace and cooperation. Therefore, we have, with God's help, shared an ongoing dialogue, building mutual understanding and trust. We recognize the differences and similarities between the Qur'an and the Bible, both of which bid us to respect the dignity of all people, to trust and submit to God's will in everything, and to work for a society of justice and peace where hate and fear are overcome by love.

As Muslims and as United Methodist Christians, we share a strong emphasis on prayer, the call for the pursuit of personal holiness and social justice, and the focus on charity and the dignity of every human being. Both Islam and Christianity are expressed in many different ways in different cultures, and yet within those differences, we recognize the faithfulness of most Muslims and Christians as they seek to live lives committed to God. We believe that God calls us to affirm the dignity and wholeness of every human being, and we respect the right of all persons to worship God in the way that is most meaningful to them.

We accept each other as persons of faith; stand firm against violence and hatred in all its forms; stand with persons who are being persecuted and are suffering for their faith; and trust in the power, grace, mercy and guidance of Almighty God.

We, as brothers and sisters within the Abrahamic family, commit ourselves to a relationship grounded in our mutual love for God and dedication to the ethical core of our faiths.

We share a mutual sense of responsibility to work together and agree to:

Continue in dialogue and expand dialogue to include our local faith communities; Work together on issues of social justice; Inform one another of situations that may affect each other's faith community; Gather annually to celebrate, reflect on our relationship, and to reaffirm our commitment to each other.[9]

In post–9/11 times, this yearly reaffirmation and celebration between two communities has increased mutual respect and interaction.

Elvira Arellano was ordered deported on August 20, 2007, for living in the United States illegally. After evading a deportation order, she took refuge at the United Methodist Church of Adalberto on Division Street in Chicago, where she remained for twelve months. There were strong supporters from various communities, but I particularly celebrated the most powerful solidarity from the Council of Islamic Organizations of Greater Chicago. They supplied thousands of bottles of water throughout the year. Such symbolic ties between United Methodist churches and Islamic communities became beautiful societal narratives in the Chicago area. As a result, many United Methodist communities got involved in interreligious relationship with neighbor Muslim communities. The impact was remarkable, both in the church and the community. Hans Küng's remarks have been our church's useful guide:

> There will be no peace among the peoples of this world without peace among the world religions. There will be no peace among the world religions without peace among the Christian churches. The community of the Church is an integral part of the world community. . . . Peace is indivisible: it begins within us. [10]

Another emphasis established in northern Illinois was an Interfaith Bus Tour for United Methodists. To deepen interfaith understanding, the Bishop's Interfaith Bus Tour was established in the Chicago area. Hundreds of United Methodist youth and adults visited the houses of other faith groups. Sites visited included Congregation Beth Shalom, the BAPS Shri Swaminarayan Mandir Complex, the Jain Society of Metropolitan Chicago, the Midwest Islamic Center, the Sikh Religious Society of Chicago, the Korean Zen Buddhist Temple, and others. The tour began on a Friday evening with Shabbat worship with the Jewish community and ended on Sunday with Holy Communion. Each interfaith encounter proved to be a rich spiritual experience, as diverse faith communities welcomed visiting Christians with great hospitality. Conversations deepened relationships between people of faith and many reported "awakening moments" of new understanding and appreciation.

THE CHANGING RELIGIOUS LANDSCAPE

The landscape of the religious field around us becomes noticeably interconnected as more families relate through interreligious marriages and adoptions. Intercultural and interreligious exchanges happen in every public sector and workplace. Our authentic claim as Christians require more open and embracing minds to other faiths and religions. Many in the United States make the assumption that the influence of religion in the world is declining since many of our congregations are declining. But the opposite is the reality. In a study completed by Gordon-Conwell Seminary, it was observed that:

> For the period 1970–2010, several global trends related to religious affiliation are apparent. In 1970, nearly 82 percent of the world's population was religious. By 2020 this had grown to around 88 percent, with a projected increase to almost 90 percent by 2020.[11]

The dynamic growth of interreligious relationships in our daily living is undeniable. Christians around the world today find themselves in contexts that are very different from those of previous generations. Proactive interfaith relationships are imperative for Christian disciples who seek to transform the world with justice, peace, and mercy.

Diana L. Eck urges churches to form working partnerships with other religious communities:

> Interreligious dialogue is a basic communication network and it has an extensive ethical and practical agenda. Terms like "peace" and "justice" will become nothing but the well-intentioned yet meaningless slogans of our separate tribes if they are not understood to involve a serious commitment toward working in partnership with people of other faiths.[12]

The bottom line: We, who are people of faith, need one another!

QUESTIONS

1. In what ways should the quest for interreligious relationships have the same priority as striving for Christian unity?

2. How are holiness and hospitality manifest in your local congregation?

3. Why should Christians participate or not participate in the rites and practices of other religions?

4. What practical steps can you or your congregation take to promote interreligious relationships?

5. Can you share how interreligious relationships have an impact on your daily life?

NOTES

1. John Wesley, "Catholic Spirit: Sermon 39," http://wesley.nnu.edu/john-wesley/the-sermons-of-john-wesley-1872-edition/sermon-39-catholic-spirit/. Accessed on 4 March 2015.

2. Hans Küng, *Christianity and the World Religions: Paths to Dialogue with Islam, Hinduism, and Buddhism* (New York: Doubleday, 1986), p. 18.

3. Ibid., p. 442.

4. "Jesus, Remember Me," sermon manuscript, delivered in Fort Worth, Texas, during General Conference, p. 2008.

5. Diana L. Eck, *Encountering God: A Spiritual Journey from Bozeman to Banaras* (Boston: Beacon Press, 1993), p. 167.

6. Ibid., p. 96.

7. E. Stanley Jones, *Christ at the Round Table* (Nashville: Abingdon Press, 1928), p. 22.

8. *The United Methodist Book of Resolutions* (Nashville: The United Methodist Publishing House, 2012), #6061, p. 800.

9. The Declaration of Relationship was signed in April 2006. http://www.ciogc.org/index.php/interfaith-relations/united-methodist.

10. Küng, *Christianity and the World Religions*, p. 443.

11. Gordon-Conwell Seminary, *Christianity in Its Global Context*, p. 6.

12. Eck, *Encountering God*, p. 202.

United Methodists prefer the risk of vigorous encounter with other living faiths to the escape of insipid interreligious separatism.

Stephen J. Sidorak, Jr., 2012

Because of the grace that God gave me, I can say to each one of you: don't think of yourself more highly than you ought to think. Instead, be reasonable since God has measured out a portion of faith to each one of you. We have many parts in one body, but the parts don't all have the same function. In the same way, though there are many of us, we are one body in Christ, and individually we belong to each other.

Romans 12:3-5

CHAPTER 5

Enhancing Christian Unity and Interreligious Relationships through Dialogue

Sudarshana Devadhar

Over the years many people have asked whether interfaith dialogue is necessary or appropriate. For over forty years that question has been posed in the ecumenical church, beginning with the heated discussion at the World Council of Churches' Fifth Assembly that met in Nairobi, Kenya, in 1975. At that time the interfaith dialogue wing of the WCC was still in its infancy. Some people claimed that dialogue led to syncretism; others argued it was a betrayal of the Christian gospel; whereas Christian delegates from some parts of the world, particularly Asia, claimed that it indeed was not just necessary, but imperative for our participation in the extension of the kingdom or reign of God on this earth.

INTERFAITH DIALOGUE AS THE NEW NORMAL

Decades ago I wrote a dissertation on the famed Indian theologian Stanley J. Samartha's ecumenical contribution to interfaith dialogue. After I defended my dissertation, a member of my examining committee, Dr. Pieter de Jong, asked me: "Suda, do you think interfaith dialogue will ever become a topic of interest in the United States?" I remember answering this question with something like, "Though this question may not be relevant today in some people's eyes, this will indeed become a key topic in the United States and all over the world, as the people of God move around the world with different faith backgrounds."

At the time the United States understood itself primarily as a nation of people who were Protestant, Catholic, or Jewish. Adherents of Islam, Buddhism, and Hinduism were relatively few and most people did not have daily encounters with persons of other faiths. In contrast, Christians in countries like India and Sri Lanka have always known what is was like to live in a multireligious community, with Christians as a decided minority. Thus, interfaith dialogue emerged outside of the Western world, as Christians like E. Stanley Jones, Stanley J. Samartha, and S. Wesley Ariarajah explored issues in interfaith relations. They were realists, not romantics; they understood dialogue was not just a quick discussion that suddenly resolved all differences. As Ariarajah writes:

> Dialogue . . . calls for serious study, analysis, discernment and the capacity to cut through the superficial and "fronts" that beguile, to arrive at the heart of the matters that divide us, and seek to face them with honesty. True dialogue is a challenging encounter; it is not for the faint-hearted.[1]

Sometimes dialogue is not even spoken but enacted. A few years after making that statement to Dr. de Jong, as a pastor I led a youth group from a church I was serving to an inner city mission church in Boston called "The Church of All Nations." While we were serving lunch to homeless people, a Hindu and a Christian were standing next to each other. Though we did not have a verbal dialogue on doctrinal, theological, or faith issues, in our own way and without naming it, we, as Christian and Hindu, were serving food together to hungry people as part of our participation in the extension work of the reign of God, fulfilling the challenge posed to us by Christ, "But strive first for the kingdom of God and his righteousness" (Matthew 6:33 NRSV).

Increasingly, interfaith activities and relationships have become the new normal, not just in Asia but around the world. Recently, I read about a pastor in Germany who was building a house of worship for Jews, Christians, and Muslims, each in their own space with commitments to their own respective faith communities, cooperating together but maintaining their own religious integrity and commitments.

All of this is happening at the same time the number of post-modern Christians, especially in the West, is growing. According to research conducted by Barna Group in the United States, Christians are becoming less biblically and theologically literate, more ingrown and less outreach oriented in witnessing to their faith. Christians are increasingly reticent to engage in faith-oriented conversations. Participation in community activities aimed at service and justice is escalating. Tolerance has increased as dogmatism has decreased. "Unparalleled theological diversity" in the church and society is anticipated for the future.[2]

Vital Congregations and the Reign of God

The United Methodist emphasis on creating vital congregations of inspiring worship, engaged disciples, effective clergy, and small-group ministries is imperative, but it should never lead to confusing the church with the kingdom or reign of God. The church plays a critical part in extending the reign of God on earth, but God's loving and liberating initiatives in the world go beyond any one denomination or even the church.

Christians and vital congregations need to invite people of God from other faiths and no faiths to participate in the reign of God. It is the need of the hour, particularly as our cities and villages become more and more postmodern in theology and practice, not just in the United States and Europe, but increasingly in other parts of the globe, including Africa, Asia, and Latin America.

Likewise, unity among Christians is vital. The scandal of Christian denominationalism is that the world and people of other faiths are bewildered by our divisions. Too often we have escalated our differences even in our own denomination, rather than finding paths of peacemaking or building bridges to connect persons who disagree. Hopefully vital congregations will be focused not only on meeting the needs of their parishioners, but reaching out in creative, compassionate, and sacrificial ways to support justice, peace, and the integrity of creation.

INTERFAITH DIALOGUE AND THE GREAT COMMISSION

Embracing interfaith dialogue does not mean abandoning witnessing of Christ's inclusive love for all people. Globally, Christians continue to fulfill their passion for the Great Commission:

> And Jesus came and said to them, "All authority in heaven and on earth has been given to me. Go therefore and make disciples of all nations, baptizing them in the name of the Father and of the Son and of the Holy Spirit, and teaching them to obey everything I have commanded you. And remember, I am with you always, to the end of the age."
>
> (Matthew 28:18-20 NRSV)

As we reflect upon the promise and challenge of interfaith dialogue for a United Methodist witness in an interreligious world where postmodern Christians are growing, we are placed in situations like the psalmist, who said, "How could we sing the LORD's song in a foreign land?" (Psalm 137:4 NRSV).

The changing global religious landscape in our own country and around the world challenges us to be faithful to the Great Commission in a new way without minimizing the power of Jesus' command, without losing its integrity, and by maintaining the unity of the church at every level. A divided church only weakens our witness and hinders the experience of the reign of God.

Though all interfaith scholars may not agree with me, interfaith dialogue, if used properly, may become one of the tools for Christian mission. Let me emphasize—it should be used as a loving instrument for Christian mission, promoting justice and peace, but not for converting a person from one faith to another. Practicing silent evangelism, for example, can be effective in fulfilling the Great Commission. Even though Mother Teresa did not preach to anyone, many came to accept Christ because of her strong Christian witness. Evangelism is very powerful when the story of Christ is shared with joy and humility.[3] In that process, persons may find a way to follow and accept the Lordship of Jesus Christ, thereby ushering the reign of God in a new way.

RESPONDING TO THREE QUESTIONS

In thinking how dialogue enhances Christian unity and interreligious relationships, three questions need a response.

First, a somber question all of us need to ask is, when Jesus asked us to "strive first for the kingdom of God and his righteousness" (Matthew 6:33 NRSV), do we consider this a monopoly of Christians only, or is it extended to people of all faiths? Read anew Matthew 6:9-14 about Jesus' teaching of the Lord's Prayer. One can say this prayer without naming the name of Jesus, which means this plea could be said by Hindu, Muslim, Jew, or Christian. In this prayer, Jesus yearns for "your kingdom come" (Matthew 6:10 NRSV). One of the ways to promote work for the extension of the kingdom of God on this earth is by inviting people of all faiths and those of no faith to join in this great ministry and mission of extending the reign of God on this earth.

One evangelical danger is that, in our excitement to increase the membership of a particular church, we sometimes proselytize members from other churches, without giving any attention to Christian discipleship. When Christian discipleship is taken seriously, the focus becomes not building a church by extinguishing other churches but by inviting people outside our churches who may not look or act like us to follow Christ. Using lessons we have learned from interfaith dialogue can be helpful in this endeavor, particularly with persons who subscribe to no faith or are suspicious, or even hostile, to particular historical religious traditions.

Second, why have churches not grown in some parts of the world? One reason churches did not grow in certain regions was that during the missionary movement of the last two centuries, when Christians were converted, they were placed in missionary compounds. They were shut off from the rest of the community and separated from previous relationships. Though mission compounds are disappearing in the twenty-first century, the placing of Christians in a separate area, thus removing them from their loved ones, hinders the opportunities for Christian witness.

Let me be quick to note that I was raised in a mission compound in India! It was only when I was studying in a theological college that I realized my many missed opportunities in gaining the trust and confidence of my friends from other faiths and the possibilities to share the gospel of Jesus Christ with people of other faiths.

I am grateful to God for the work of Christian missionaries without whom my ancestors would not have embraced Christianity. Considerable social reform would not have occurred without some of the Christian initiatives and institutions. However, in spreading the gospel, some of the indigenous cultural values and symbols that people embraced were rejected without consideration and respect for the people. Thus it weakened the Christian witness in some parts of the world. As the gospel was taken to the southern hemisphere, mostly by the missionaries from the northern hemisphere in the nineteenth and twentieth centuries, a great missiologist, D. T. Niles of Sri Lanka, eloquently wrote:

> The Gospel is a seed which, when it is sown in the soil of the country's life, brings forth a plant. The plant is Christianity. It bears the marks both of the seed and of the soil. There is only one Gospel, but there are many Christianities, many cultural forms in which men express their Christian faith. It is inevitable that the missionary should bring a potted plant, the Christianity of his own culture; it is essential that he allow the pot to be broken and the plant to be rooted in the soil of the country to which he goes.[4]

Thus, it is always important to consider whether our invitation to people to join with us in the extension work of the reign of God is rooted firmly in the soil of the area, or are our communications only on the surface? To say it more clearly, before we invite a person of another faith, or no faith, in this bold task, are we grounded in our own Scriptures? Do we understand the doctrines of our own faith? Do we have a clear sense of what it means to sing the song of the Lord in a strange land where postmodern Christianity is growing? Do we know what it means to glorify our God without offending a neighbor, yet demonstrating to him or her silently through our lives and without preaching that we are followers of Jesus Christ? What is our understanding and dependence of the power of the Holy Spirit in our mission and all our ministries? Do we trust the Holy Spirit to lead us in this endeavor, even by rejecting all our egos and pride in this process? Do we understand what it means when we sing a verse from Charles Wesley's hymn "to serve the present age"?[5] Do we understand what prevenient grace means in our Wesleyan understanding?

Third, are we willing to honestly study the faiths of our neighbors before we enter into dialogue with them? This calls for research to understand where persons of differing religious convictions come from in terms of their culture and belief. What are their core convictions and why? What are their dietary restrictions and religious symbols? Being aware and informed enhances meaningful dialogue.

Likewise when there are conflicts and disagreements within United Methodism, are we willing to honestly seek to understand the positions of others before we enter into dialogue with them? And are we willing to learn as we listen? And even be open to the Holy Spirit changing our minds and hearts?

An Amish proverb says, "Before we can pray 'Thy Kingdom come,' we must pray 'My kingdom go.'"[6] A true dialogue will not take place unless we are willing to give up our own kingdoms of arrogance, power, and superiority.

PREPARING OURSELVES FOR DIALOGUE

Christians entering into interfaith dialogue need first to understand their own faith and be prepared to explain historic doctrinal and scriptural perspectives. Personally, I argue that anyone attempting to promote interfaith dialogue should have a clear understanding and experience of our triune God: God the Father, God the Son, and God the Holy Spirit.

Second, we are called to have a thorough and accurate knowledge of the sacred texts used by Christians. Our holistic Bible study must be historical, critical, and contextual. It dare not be narrow, lest we misrepresent the fullness and complexity of the Scriptures.

Third, a deep and meaningful prayer life is imperative for effective interfaith dialogue. We cannot enter into interfaith dialogue until we are soaked in prayer, asking God to fill us with divine power, the compassionate love of Christ, and the presence of the Holy Spirit. People of other religious persuasions pray regularly and faithfully, engage in meditation, and seek divine guidance.

AN INTRAFAITH DIALOGUE

John Wesley spoke of Christian conferencing, sometimes now referred to as "Holy Conferencing." For John Wesley, conferencing was a means of grace—a way of experiencing God's great love in our lives.

Interfaith dialogue and Christian conferencing are two key approaches to enhancing Christian unity and interreligious relationships. Related but different, each method recognizes and affirms the *imago dei* (image of God) within every human being; respectfully recognizes, understands, and appreciates religious similarities; and seeks to overcome differences wherever possible without betraying belief.

Lessons learned from decades of interfaith dialogue can now be usefully implemented in intrafaith dialogue (that is, among members of the same denomination when they disagree). What once seemed only a practice to be employed among Christians in Asia now is imperative for us all. We can benefit from the experience of the ecumenical church as we seek to maintain the unity Christ wills for our communion.

QUESTIONS

1. Why has interfaith dialogue been controversial among Christians?

2. How is interfaith dialogue the new normal?

3. What would it mean for Christians to invite persons of other faiths to join in seeking the kingdom or reign of God on earth?

4. Are interfaith dialogue and fulfilling the Great Commission contradictory?

5. How can Christian or holy conferencing be helpful in dealing with church conflicts and controversies?

Notes

1. S. Wesley Ariarajah, *Not Without My Neighbour: Issues in Interfaith Relations* (Geneva: World Council of Churches, 1999), p. 24. See also Sudarshana Devadhar's unpublished Ph.D. dissertation, *Stanley J. Samartha's Contribution to the Interfaith Dialogue*, submitted to Drew University, Madison, New Jersey, 1987.

2. Barna Group research published December 13, 2010; https://www.barna.org/culture-articles/462-six-megathemes-emerge-from-2010.

3. See Sudarshana Devadhar, "Is Samartha's Concept Relevant to the Christian Mission in North America?" Unpublished paper at Oxford Institute, 2001.

4. Daniel Thambyrajah (D. T.) Niles, *That They May Have Life* (New York: Harper, 1951), p. 80.

5. Charles Wesley, "A Charge to Keep I Have," *The United Methodist Hymnal* (Nashville: The United Methodist Publishing House, 1989), 413, stanza 2.

6. Suzanne Woods Fisher, *Amish Peace: Simple Wisdom for a Complicated World* (Grand Rapids: Baker Books, 2009), p. 211.

We live in a time of global crises. Economic, ecological, socio-political and spiritual challenges confront us. In darkness and in the shadow of death, in suffering and persecution, how precious is the gift of hope from the Risen Lord! By the flame of the Spirit in our hearts, we pray to Christ to brighten the world: for his light to turn our whole beings to caring for the whole of creation and to affirm that all people are created in God's image. Listening to voices that often come from the margins, let us all share lessons of hope and perseverance. Let us recommit ourselves to work for liberation and to act in solidarity. May the illuminating Word of God guide us on our journey. God of life, lead us to justice and peace!

Message of the 10th Assembly of the WCC,
Busan, South Korea, November 2013

Then they will reply, "Lord, when did we see you hungry or thirsty or a stranger or naked or sick or in prison and didn't do anything to help you?" Then he will answer, "I assure you that when you haven't done it for one of the least of these, you haven't done it for me."

Matthew 25:44-45

CHAPTER 6

Envisioning an Abundant Life for All God's Creation

Gaspar João Domingos

and

Gladys P. Mangiduyos

Twenty-two thousand children die each day due to poverty. Jesus said, "Let the little children come unto me" (Matthew 19:14 NRSV), but today children are the forgotten of the earth. As a report from the United Nations International Children's Emergency Fund (UNICEF) says, they "die quietly in some of the poorest villages on earth, far removed from the scrutiny and the conscience of the world. Being meek and weak in life makes these dying multitudes even more invisible in death."[1]

As United Methodists who live in Africa and Asia, we are painfully aware of the one-sixth of humanity who live in extreme poverty. Some 850 million people in the world do not have enough food to lead a healthy, active life. That's about one in nine people on earth.

We grieve that nearly a billion people entered the twenty-first century unable to read a book or sign their names. We grieve that many people lack basic clean water and sanitary conditions.

Ending poverty in our lifetime is integral to our commitment to enhancing Christian unity and improving interreligious relationships. Every dollar squandered on unnecessary quarrels between persons of faith is money that could have cooperatively been used to combat hunger, disease, and poverty. The familiar African proverb asserts that "it takes a whole village to raise a child." Children could live and be educated and attain their potential if our villages and communities of faith were focused on their well-being and not divided in ways that yield death, not life.

The Mesh of Challenges

The great hope that Jesus promises in John 10:10 is that "I came that they may have life, and have it abundantly" (NRSV). But he warns that "the thief comes only to steal and kill and destroy." In the twenty-first century, clearly the thieves are poverty, hunger, and disease that steal, kill, and destroy.

The United Methodist Church has made global health a priority, as infectious diseases continue to blight the lives of the poor across the world. An estimated 40 million people are living with HIV/AIDS, with millions of deaths every year. "Every year there are 350 [to] 500 million cases of malaria, with 1 million fatalities: Africa accounts for 90 percent of malarial deaths and African children account for over 80 percent of malaria victims worldwide."[2]

Combating poverty and poor health requires maximum resources and commitment. Our church alone cannot meet all the needs, but unless we are involved as a people of faith, poverty can never be ended. Our efforts are strengthened when we work ecumenically and interreligiously for the welfare of all in the community.

Poverty is not one challenge but a mesh of challenges that interact with each other. Its causes are multifactorial and multidimensional.[3]

It is experienced in various degrees through different dimensions, demography, geography, and time. This includes about 4.4 billion people living in developing countries of which three-fifths lack basic sanitation, one-third have no access to clean water, one-fourth do not have adequate housing, and one-fifth have no access to modern health services.

The World Bank notes that poverty involves not only personal and financial insecurity, but social and political disempowerment. It has an impact not just on income, but education and health, including life expectancy.[4] Different age groups are affected, with the very young and old suffering severely. Women inevitably live with less.

In a twenty-first-century world of great prosperity, abundant food, life-giving medicines, and great technology, we yet witness scandalous depths of global poverty, hunger, disease, and violence. The gap between the rich and the poor—even in our church—is better described as a chasm or canyon, demeaning human life and hampering our mission and ministry in the world.

THE DRY BONES OF A WORLD IN RUINS

Ezekiel's vision of the valley of dry bones is a familiar and vivid Old Testament passage. The Lord shows to the prophet Ezekiel a mesh of misery, a world laid in ruins, a valley of dry bones lacking any sign of life. The Lord led Ezekiel on a tour and told him, "Prophesy to these bones, and say to them: O dry bones, hear the word of the LORD." And the Lord God promises: "I will cause breath to enter you, and you shall live." So Ezekiel did as he was commanded and prophesied. "Suddenly there was a noise, a rattling, and the bones came together, bone to its bone. I looked, and there were sinews on them, and flesh had come upon them, and skin had covered them; but there was no breath in them." But then God's "breath came into them, and they lived, and stood on their feet, a vast multitude" (see Ezekiel 37:1-10 NRSV).

Millions in today's world feel as if they are living amid a barren landscape of dry and dead bones with no hope in sight. They identify, however, with words of Scripture that promise: "O my people . . . I will put my spirit within you and you shall live" (verses 13-14). Dry bones are highly symbolic language, for they are the framework of the human body. The nineteenth-century spiritual called "Dem Bones" created by African American slaves used this imagery to express their faith in a God who can bring hope and health even amid life's cruelty and misery.

What are urgently needed today are ecumenical and interfaith prophets like Ezekiel who will speak out against the injustice and inequalities of the world. We need Christian communities of faith for whom ending poverty and disease are not peripheral to their ministry but a priority of their mission.

BEYOND GREED

The father of the Filipino author of this chapter used to say, "Behind the twisted norm of inequality is the greed of capitalism." India's Mahatma Gandhi counseled, "There is a sufficiency in the world for man's need but not for man's greed." This greed has caused the prevailing absence of abundance for all God's children.

Critics of capitalism like Colin Todhunter claim "capitalism is based on addiction. It encourages people to crave for more and more wealth and more and more products," resulting in "war, exploitation, and the immiseration of working folk." This framework of dry bones is "ultimately ruinous for the individual, humankind and the environment."[5] Even criticizing the greed of capitalism we understand can be controversial, since as the Angolan proverb warns: "The mouse does not talk back to the lion."

Edward Bernays, the father of advertising, propaganda, and public relations, knew how to manipulate the pleasure and pain centers of the brain and how to get the masses hooked on the products of capitalism. This manipulation has been developed and perfected over the past century or so, and we are all subjected to it each and every day. Capitalism does not want a well-informed, educated populace that is aware of its disfranchisement, exploitation, and manipulation. It does not require disenchantment and revolutionary murmurs, but acquiescence and passivity.

Todhunter claims: "The state provision of welfare, education, health services, and the role of the public sector are undermined by the market constituting the best method for supplying human needs and protecting the environment. Nothing must be allowed to stop the raping of the land because this is deemed positive, this is 'growth.' The hallowed 'greed is good' persists."[6] Much of this indoctrination all too often goes unnoticed. Cynicism and apathy can take hold: this is the way of the world and nothing can or should be done about it. This framework prevents people seeking out emancipatory alternatives. Sometimes we are not even open to having our dry bones experience God's breath of new life and hope.

Alleviating the misery and suffering of this world is a far-reaching endeavor. A century of hard educational endeavor is surely not enough. What kind of ecumenical leadership do we need to nurture? How do we lessen the miseries of the world where arrogance and greed are so pervasive? Where people uphold fallacy and bigotry? Where almost everybody embraces callousness and insensitivities? How do we enable these bones in ruins to be restored and have life? How do we as churches give life? Can these bones live?

THE GIFT OF INCLUSIVITY AND ABUNDANCE

The inclusiveness of the church is a hallmark of United Methodism. The Constitution (Article IV) clearly states that "The United Methodist Church is a part of the church universal, which is one Body in Christ." It emphasizes that all should be included saying "all persons are of sacred worth" and none should be excluded because of "race, color, national origin, status, or economic condition."[7] Inclusiveness challenges us to an attitude of humility, an attitude of tolerance, an attitude of learning, an attitude of fidelity. It sets a basis for equality that seeks an abundant life for all God's creation.

The abundant life of which Jesus spoke is spiritual as well as material. In the face of the despair of dry bones, Christians remain hopeful and joyful persons. We are grateful for the air we breathe and the relationships we share. Christians in Africa, Asia, and Latin America display remarkably positive attitudes and express enthusiasm in living, despite difficulties. Though being pressed in by poverty and facing death on a daily basis, they believe in the power of Jesus Christ and are thankful for God's gifts of inclusiveness and abundance.

Some religious groups try to avert the eyes of believers from injustice and inequality, but United Methodists do not just raise our eyes to heaven, for we know the earth is the place we are called to work. While we seek the abundant spiritual and material life for all— regardless of their religious persuasion—we urge people to not be angry for anger's sake. Rage and fury only harm the believer's life. Instead let our anger be directed toward those persons, policies, systems, and structures that deny human rights, entrench corruption, steal from the poor, reinforce poverty, encourage violence, prohibit peace, and deepen poverty—all ways that limit the abundant life.

SEEKING THE ABUNDANT LIFE

Everyone has the right to a standard of living adequate for the health and well-being of oneself or one's family, including food, clothing, housing and medical care, and necessary social services. Everyone has the right to live with dignity.

The United Methodist Social Principles[8] stipulate that "ways must be found to share more equitably the resources of the world." It decries "exploitative economic practices" that make "poverty self-perpetuating." Our church's stance reflects Christ's teachings for the poor and marginalized. Our social teachings proclaim:

> As a church, we are called to support the poor and challenge the rich. To begin to alleviate poverty, we support such policies as: adequate income maintenance, quality education, decent housing,

job training, meaningful employment opportunities, adequate medical and hospital care, humanization and radical revisions of welfare programs, work for peace in conflict areas and efforts to protect creation's integrity. Since low wages are often a cause of poverty, employers should pay their employees a wage that does not require them to depend upon government subsidies such as food stamps or welfare for their livelihood.[9]

United Methodists, through our ecumenical work and interreligious relationships, seek to alleviate suffering and eradicate causes of injustices and all that robs life of dignity and worth. Our goal is to facilitate the development of full human potential and share in the building of global community through the church universal. In our quest for Christian unity and interreligious relationships, we must beware of ethnocentric sin and seek God's grace and humility.

Required is establishing a culture of fair-minded critical thought. With the ruinous system of capitalism everywhere, becoming critical of the system is a good start. It will help establish a culture of fair-minded critical thought.

The Challenge

Envisioning a strengthened Christian witness and expanded global involvement, building partnerships, participating in interfaith dialogue, and encouraging Christian unity around the world require firm grounding in our Christian faith. Critical is educating Christian leaders who are committed to ecumenical and interreligious values and who courageously offer prophetic voices for justice and equality. It is crucial to educate human capital because people are the very foundation of a stable society.

John Wesley emphasized education and encouraged ministry with the poor. He wrote, "To have a vibrant and sound faith one must be able to read and write ably and to think and reason critically." In 1748, he said, "Education should be considered in no other light than as the art of recovering [persons] to [their] rational perfection

. . . teaching them how to think, judge, and act."[10] The function of education is to teach one to think intensely, and to think critically. In the words of Martin Luther King, Jr., "Intelligence plus character— that is the goal of true education."[11]

United Methodists always have affirmed that education is a key to unlocking human potential and finding future ways of securing an abundant life for all. As a denomination, along with improving global health, we have a high priority on educating persons for leadership in church and society through our schools, seminaries, colleges, and universities. In doing so, we trust our Christian leaders will work for the common good, strive toward unity, and respect all of God's creation.

Global problems will increase and the abundant life will escape the masses if the twisted norms of injustice and inequality persist. United Methodists are challenged to live up to the simple rules set forth by John Wesley: "Do no harm, do good, and stay in love with God."[12] And in our ecumenical and interfaith activities, let us always remember the words of Jeremiah: "He defended the rights of the poor and needy; then it went well. Isn't that what it means to know me? declares the LORD" (Jeremiah 22:16).

QUESTIONS

1. In what ways and how often does your church address issues of global poverty?

2. How do you think the suffering of the impoverished in the world can be alleviated?

3. What does it mean to say inclusiveness is "a hallmark of United Methodism"?

4. How can greater Christian unity and more positive interreligious relationships lead to the "life abundant" promised by Jesus?

NOTES

1. See http://www.unicef.org/pon00/immu1.htm.

2. See http://www.globalissues.org/article/26/poverty-facts-and-stats.

3. According to Paraso (2014).

4. World Bank, "Understanding Different Dimensions of Poverty," see http://web.worldbank.org/WEBSITE/EXTERNAL/TOPICS/EXTURBAN DEVELOPMENT/EXTURBANPOVERTY/O,,contentMDK:20276602 ~menuPK:7173807~pagePK:148956~piPK:216618~theSitePK:3413525 ~isCURL:Y,00.html.

5. Colin Todhunter, "Craving for More and More Wealth, Refusing Capitalism," September 19, 2012, http://www.globalresearch.ca/craving -for-more-and-more-wealth-refusing-capitalism/5305102.

6. Ibid.

7. *The Book of Discipline of The United Methodist Church* (Nashville: The United Methodist Publishing House, 2012), p. 24.

8. *The Discipline*, Social Principles, ¶163. IV. The Economic Community, *E) Poverty*; p. 130.

9. Ibid.

10. John Wesley, Sermon 95, "On the Education of Children," http:// wesley.nnu.edu/john-wesley/the-sermons-of-john-wesley-1872-edition /sermon-95-on-the-education-of-children/.

11. Martin Luther King, Jr., "The Purpose of Education," Morehouse College student paper, The Maroon Tiger, 1947. http://www.washingtonpost .com/blogs/answer-sheet/wp/2014/01/20/mlk-intelligence-plus-character -that-is-the-goal-of-true-education/.

12. John Wesley's three simple rules were: First, "Do No Harm"; Second, "Do Good"; Third, "Attend all of the Ordinances of God," or as Bishop Rueben Job paraphrased it: "Stay in Love with God."

"*A test of our* koinonia *is how we live with those with whom we disagree.*"

Fifth World Conference on Faith and Order
Santiago de Compostela

Therefore, as a prisoner for the Lord, I encourage you to live as people worthy of the call you received from God. Conduct yourselves with all humility, gentleness, and patence. Accept each other with love, and make an effort to preserve the unity of the Spirit with the peace that ties you together. You are one body and one spirit, just as God also called you in one hope. There is one Lord, one faith, one baptism, and one God and Father of all who is over all, through all, and in all.

Ephesians 4:1-6

CHAPTER 7

FINDING A WAY FORWARD
FOR A *UNITED* METHODIST
CHURCH

ADAM HAMILTON

We stand at a crossroads in The United Methodist Church. The ongoing debate over homosexuality continues to divide us. It consumes a great deal of our energy, energy we are diverting from our core mission of "making disciples of Jesus Christ for the transformation of the world." United Methodists agree that we are to love gay and lesbian people. We also agree that the Bible has authority in our lives and churches. We disagree on whether the biblical passages that speak of same-sex intimacy reflect God's timeless will, or, like some other passages, reflect the cultural and moral sensitivities of the biblical authors and their times.

In the United States, few doubt that the number of states allowing for same-sex marriage will continue to increase. Nor that public support for the right of gay and lesbian people to marry will continue to grow at a rapid pace.[1] Two-thirds of young adults support the right of same-sex couples to marry. The church does not determine its positions based upon legal realities and public opinion polls, but these trends make clear that the debate about homosexuality within the church is not going away.

We believe the issue of homosexuality should not be the cause for dividing The United Methodist Church.[2] There are faithful people on both sides of this divide, within the same conference, congregation, and even family. There are United Methodist Christians who have a high view of Scripture, who are theologically orthodox and committed Wesleyans on both sides of the issue. Within families, congregations, and annual conferences we have learned to live with our diversity. While some on both sides of the divide believe the only way forward for the church is schism, we believe schism diminishes the witness and vitality of the entire church. We think there is a better way.

THE LOCAL CHURCH AS THE LOCUS OF DISCIPLE-MAKING

The Book of Discipline of The United Methodist Church, 2012, notes that the local church is the "most significant arena through which disciple-making occurs." It is "primarily at the level of the [local] charge . . . that the church encounters the world," and "the local church is a strategic base from which Christians move out to the structures of society." "Each local church shall have a definite evangelistic, nurture, and witness responsibility for its members and the surrounding area. . . . It shall be responsible for ministering to all its members."[3]

Ministry with gay and lesbian people, their family and friends, occurs in local churches, not at annual conferences and not at the General Conference level. Likewise the interpretation of Scripture regarding homosexuality happens, for most United Methodists, not at General Conference, but in Sunday school classes, in Bible studies, and in the context of worship in their local churches. Outreach to the community, evangelism, nurture, and witness must occur out of local churches, and it will look different for each congregation.

If the local church is the locus of most United Methodist ministry in the world, we believe it should be at the local church level that United Methodists discern how they will minister with and to gay and lesbian people in their community. Currently about 850 General Conference delegates from around the world, in vastly different contexts, gather to vote to determine how *all* United Methodists must interpret Scripture on this issue and what local congregations can or cannot do in ministry with gay and lesbian people. Every four years we go through this same exercise and we leave General Conference more divided than ever. What a gift it would be to the church if the General Conference were able to focus on what unites us, not what divides, and on the critical needs of the world and the church.

Local church pastors currently decide whether they will or will not marry a couple. Likewise, local churches currently set the policies for weddings that occur in their buildings. We believe that one way forward regarding the issue of same-sex marriage would be to allow local church pastors to determine if they are willing to officiate at same-sex marriages and to allow the church council or administrative board of local churches to determine if they will host same-sex marriages in their facilities.

PROTECTING THE RIGHTS OF LOCAL CHURCHES TO HOLD THEIR OWN CONVICTIONS

In order to maintain the unity of the Church while allowing for different practices regarding same-sex marriage, the rights of traditionalist churches and pastors to interpret Scripture as they do and progressive pastors and churches to interpret as they do must be protected. This will be a challenge for both sides.

Traditionalists believe that same-sex relationships are explicitly forbidden by Scripture and are not God's will. To ask them to compromise on this issue in their own practice feels to them like asking them to embrace other forms of immorality. Progressives believe that same-sex marriage is a human rights issue, that the Scriptures related to same-sex relationships are similar to Scriptures affirming slavery, or the subordination of women, and that the church must speak against discrimination and injustice. Allowing parts of the church to continue to hold to a traditionalist view feels like asking them to affirm injustice and bigotry.

If we are to remain one Church, both sides must be willing to compromise—to allow that a case can be made for the view opposite of their own and that well-meaning, thoughtful United Methodist Christians might reach conclusions other than their own. This is very hard for passionate persons on both sides of this debate.

While it is hard to imagine compromise for many pastors, we already see this kind of compromise taking place in nearly every United Methodist church. The laity already practice this as they allow for persons in their Sunday school classes and Bible studies to hold differing views from their own. In the most conservative of churches there are laity who disagree with their pastors on this issue. In the most progressive churches there are laity who disagree with their pastors on this issue. Perhaps this is why 91 percent of United Methodist laity surveyed do not believe the church should divide over this issue.

OBJECTIONS TO LOCAL CHURCH AUTONOMY REGARDING SAME-SEX MARRIAGE

It has been argued by some that to allow local church pastors and local congregations to determine their own policies regarding same-sex marriage undermines connectionalism. We think this is a straw man argument. Connectionalism existed for two centuries before the current language related to same-sex relationships was inserted into the *Discipline*. Connectionalism does not require uniformity on all social issues, nor concurrence on all matters of biblical interpretation. Same-sex marriage is not a part of our Articles of Religion.

The seven essential elements of connectionalism are our (1) system for appointing clergy, (2) shared mission and ministry funded through the apportionment system, (3) *Trust Clause* that maintains that all United Methodist property is held in trust "for the benefit of the entire denomination,"[4] (4) episcopal system and the role bishops play in the church, (5) General Conference by which United Methodists interpret the *Discipline* and determine our shared mission, (6) common *Discipline* and *Resolutions*, and (7) common doctrinal positions and social principles.

Again some have argued that allowing for different practices among local churches and among pastors regarding same-sex marriage would make it virtually impossible for bishops to assign clergy. Once again we feel this is a "straw man." Bishops currently have churches that are reconciling and that advocate for the rights of same-sex couples to marry. They have other churches that are very conservative on this and a number of other issues. Bishops currently have pastors who are strong advocates for same-sex marriage and others who strongly oppose this. Effective bishops already take these differences into account when assigning clergy.

Some have argued that allowing local churches and their pastors to determine their own wedding policies will only push the rancorous debate about same-sex marriage from the General Conference to every United Methodist church. Yet this debate is already happening in our local churches. This allows local churches to determine their own policies rather than having 850 people from around the world determine their policies. We believe an appropriate process can be adopted whereby local churches can study the issue and determine their own policies with appropriate pastoral leadership—one that keeps a clear eye to maintaining "the unity of the Spirit in the bond of peace" (Ephesians 4:3 NRSV).

Some have suggested that a shortcoming of the "local church option" is that it requires every local church to vote on this issue. We don't believe that is true. We are suggesting that the current disciplinary language would be the *de facto* position of each United Methodist church and only those who feel strongly about changing this position would vote to change their own local church wedding policies allowing for same-sex marriage. If a local church is generally satisfied with this position, they would do nothing and retain the current language. While our proposal would not require most churches to vote, almost *every other proposal for addressing the current divide would require each church to vote.*

The proposal for "amicable separation" would require local churches to vote as to whether they join a new denomination or remain in the current denomination. This is a much larger and potentially more divisive decision. The "jurisdictional proposal" would likewise require each local church to vote as to which jurisdiction they would be a part of. Both the vote to separate or stay and the vote regarding which new jurisdiction to join would really be votes about a local church's position on same-sex marriage. Only the local church option allows most churches to take no vote at all unless and until they were ready to change the current disciplinary prohibitions against same-sex marriage.

We support the development of resources to help those local churches who wish to study these issues further; resources that will help both sides in this divide present their best case for their position. We also suggest a clear process be developed with guidelines for local churches, pastors, superintendents, and bishops that carefully work to lessen the likelihood of splits at the local church level.

WHAT IT MEANS TO BE UNITED METHODIST

United Methodist congregations currently hold different views on how to interpret the Scriptures related to homosexuality and different ways of being in ministry with gay and lesbian people. What makes us all United Methodists is not unanimity in our understanding of same-sex marriage, but rather a core set of theological, missional, and ministry convictions and practices.

To be United Methodist is to hold together a passionate and personal evangelical gospel *and* a serious and sacrificial social gospel.

It is to hold together a deep and wide understanding of grace *and* a call to holiness of heart and life. It is to hold together a faith that speaks to the intellect *and* a faith that warms the heart. To be United Methodist is to be people who study and seek to live Scripture *and* who read it with the help of tradition, experience, and reason. To be United Methodist is to invite the Spirit's sanctifying work in our lives to the end that we might love God with all that is within us *and* love our neighbors as we love ourselves.

United Methodists believe that God's grace is available to all, not only a predestined "elect." We believe that God brings good from evil, but we don't believe that God causes evil. We believe that it's okay to ask questions and that we're not meant to check our brains at the door of the church (we were, after all, started by an Oxford professor-turned-evangelist). We find helpful those guidelines we call the General Rules: Refrain from evil, do all the good you can, and do those things that help you grow in love for God. We find the Covenant Prayer a powerful reminder of what it means to call Jesus Christ Lord: "I am no longer my own, but thine. Put me to what thou wilt."[5]

United Methodists have at times been called *progressive evangelicals*. We have been seen as people of the radical or extreme center, holding together the best of the two sides of the theological divide. It is this ability to hold together the important insights and perspectives of both the left and the right that is exemplified in a church that allows local congregations to hold varied scriptural interpretations on the issue of homosexuality.

A VISION FOR THE FUTURE

We believe the world needs a vital United Methodist Church. In an increasingly secular age, the world needs churches that can make an intellectually sound case for the gospel, proclaim a faith that touches the heart, and call Christians to action seeking to help our world look more like the kingdom of God. A vital United

Methodism will remember its heritage and mission. It will also help gifted young adults answer God's call to full-time Christian service.

We believe that for United Methodism to be vital in the future we must help gifted young adults hear God's call and empower, equip, and inspire them to renew existing churches and start new ministries and congregations to reach those who are not actively involved in a church.

United Methodists have an approach to the gospel that twenty-first-century young adults find compelling. With tens of thousands of churches around the world, and freed from endless debate at the general church and annual conference level concerning homosexuality, our hope is that United Methodists might be united around our common heritage, and theological and missional convictions, to once again "spread scriptural holiness across the land."

QUESTIONS

1. How is The United Methodist Church "at a crossroads" because of the ongoing debate over sexuality?

2. Who should determine how local churches minister to gay and lesbian persons and why?

3. Can compromise be ethically and theologically justifiable to avoid schism? Why or why not?

4. Would "amicable separation" be an acceptable form of church schism?

5. What is the "way forward" for United Methodists regarding disagreements about the ordination of gay, lesbian, bisexual, and transgender persons?

Notes

1. A February 2014 Pew Research Center poll found that 52 percent of Americans now support the right for gay and lesbian people to marry, up from 31 percent just ten years ago. See http://features.pewforum.org/same -sex-marriage-attitudes/index.php.

2. Hamilton uses "we" in this chapter since the chapter was written with editorial input from David McAlister-Wilson, a group of large-church pastors, and other United Methodist leaders.

3. *The Book of Discipline of The United Methodist Church*, 2012, paragraphs 201-204

4. *Ibid.*, paragraph 2501.

5. "A Covenant Prayer in the Wesleyan Tradition," *The United Methodist Hymnal* (Nashville: The United Methodist Publishing House, 1989), 607.

"Holy conferencing is what we call the spirit and principles that guide us to be caring in our conversations—that is what makes them holy. . . . It is more than just being nice to each other around divisive issues. We find ourselves reaching deep into our souls as we seek to follow the gospel message of loving our neighbors and our enemies, including those who disagree with us with as much passion and conviction in their viewpoint as we have in ours."

Bishop Sally Dyck, 2012

Look at how good and pleasing it is
when families live together as one!

Psalm 133:1

CHAPTER 8

Where Do We Go
from Here?

Donald E. Messer

The quest for Christian unity and positive interreligious relationships proves to be both timeless and timely. Timeless since Christians have always struggled to overcome human differences to express the unity Christ wills for his church, and misunderstanding and mistrust between different religions have too often led to painful conflicts and even crusades. Timely because the latest headlines threaten potential church schism due to deep disagreements over homosexuality and the media reports that extremists are using religion to justify violence and wars.

But because we celebrate God's inclusive and unconditional love in Jesus Christ, Christians persist in bridging differences and exploring ways to enhance religious understanding among persons and communities. United Methodists have historically been known around the world as persons of faith who have transcended doctrinal differences and religious practices and found ways to bring people together. As United Methodist Bishops Wenner, Brown, and Ough noted in their opening chapter:

Seeking and maintaining Christian unity and interreligious relationships are not options, but theological obligations of our faith because we affirm a God of love and follow Jesus, the Christ, who transcended narrowness of spirit and always pressed for greater inclusivity.

At a critical point of crisis and controversy in the civil rights struggle in the United States, Martin Luther King, Jr., wrote his last book entitled *Where Do We Go from Here: Chaos or Community?*[1] In it he offered prophetic counsel that has proved both timeless and timely. He noted we live in "a great world house" in which "we have to live together" as black and white, Easterner and Westerner, Gentile and Jew, Catholic and Protestant, Moslem and Hindu" in peace, lest we "perish as fools."[2] He called on people to move beyond religious parochialism and embrace ecumenism, asserting that love is a "Hindu-Moslem-Christian-Jewish-Buddhist belief about ultimate reality."[3] King says this is best expressed in the First Letter of John:

> Beloved, let us love one another, because love is from God; everyone who loves is born of God and knows God. Whoever does not love does not know God, for God is love. . . . if we love one another, God lives in us, and his love is perfected in us. (1 John 4:7-8, 12b NSRV)

Indeed love is timeless and timely; in the apostle Paul's words: "It bears all things, believes all things, hopes all things, endures all things" (1 Corinthians 13:7 NRSV).

THE UNIVERSAL OR "CATHOLIC" SPIRIT OF JOHN WESLEY

Love of God and humanity has prompted United Methodists to be champions of ecumenism and interfaith relationships. As Bishop Mary Ann Swenson and Stephen Sidorak and other authors have noted, Wesley's sermon "Catholic Spirit" (Sermon 39) is fundamental to the Wesleyan way. Wesley recalled a kind of interfaith conversation recorded in Second Kings between Jehu and Jehonadab, a fanatical Yahwist and the founder of an extremist sect opposed to the sedentary culture of the Canaanites. Though the two men represent opposing perspectives, Jehu asks: "Is thine heart right, as my heart is with thy heart?" And Jehonadab answers: "It is." "If it be, then give me thine hand" (2 Kings 10:15 KJV).

Commenting on this text, Wesley asserted that persons will reflect different minds in religion as well as in everyday life. "So it has been from the beginning of the world, and so it will be 'till the restitution of all things.'" Wesley recognized the fallibility of all human thinking, including the differing ways persons worship. Instead of being dogmatic, Wesley was dialogical, saying: "We must both act as each is fully persuaded in his own mind. Hold you fast that which you believe is most acceptable to God, and I will do the same." A high point of the universal love theology for interfaith relations comes when Wesley adds:

> Love me not in word only, but in deed and in truth. So far as in conscience thou canst (retaining still thine own opinions, and thy own manner of worshipping God) join with me in the work of God, and let us go on hand in hand. . . . Speak honourably wherever thou art, of the work of God, by whomsoever he works, and kindly of his messengers.

Wesley's eighteenth-century words fit the contemporary context of dialogue, as urged earlier in this book by Bishops Hee-Soo Jung and Sudarshana Devadhar, both of whom contended one could be loyal to Christ while affirming one's neighbor of a different denomination or religion. Wesley preached:

> While he is steadily fixed in his religious principles in what he believes to be the truth as it is in Jesus; while he firmly adheres to that worship of God which he judges to be the most acceptable in his sight; and while he is united in the tenderest and closest ties to one particular congregation,—his heart is enlarged toward all mankind, those he knows and those he does not; he embraces with strong and cordial affection neighbours and strangers, friends and enemies. This is catholic or universal love. And he that has this is of a catholic

spirit. For love alone gives the title to this character: catholic love is a catholic spirit.[4]

DIALOGIANS OF THE FAITH

In the twenty-first century, Christians are called to be not only theologians, but also dialogians of the faith. Dialogue has replaced monologue, just as dialogue has replaced diatribe.[5] Listening and learning are as important as witnessing and sharing. Risk is involved, since genuine conversation seeks deeper understanding and the continuing revelation of the Holy Spirit. The conversion of any person may occur in the process because honest dialogians of the faith remain open to change as truth leads. The potentiality for new life and vision always exists as people seek to discover God's liberating love in their lives. As the Church of South India bishop, Lesslie Newbigen, once said, "A dialogue that is safe from all possible risks is no true dialogue."[6]

Two authors in this book—from Angola and the Philippines—have reminded us of the perils and possibilities in today's world. Lamenting the "dry bones" facing the impoverished of the earth, Bishop Gaspar João Domingos and Gladys P. Mangiduyos remind us of our responsibility for helping all God's people to attain the "abundant life" promised by Jesus Christ. Intrafaith and interfaith dialogue is imperative in the world if we are to ever overcome Christian disunity and interreligious conflict—both of which impede the abundant life that is a right for all people.

Many people of faith resist ecumenical efforts and interfaith relationships. They prefer living in the silos of their traditions and tribes. They refuse to believe anyone else could experience God or Christ in as meaningful or vibrant ways as do they. Everyone should see things the way they see them—as if one can only see a beautiful sunset over a snow-capped Colorado Rockies mountain range from just one cabin window, not on the deck or in the backyard.

My own exposure to persons of other world faiths began at age twenty when I left Dakota Wesleyan University to study at Madras Christian College in southern India. My yearlong journey abroad helped me begin to overcome my parochial perspectives and to discover for the first time the variety of religious expressions in the world. One cannot live in the homes of Muslim, Buddhist, and Hindu friends and not realize that God, in different ways and in distinct expressions, touches with love all peoples of all religions in all cultures.

During that same journey, I also came to understand that denominationalism is a scandal to the world and a sin before God! During the Christmas holidays I stayed in the Muslim home of a college friend in Sri Lanka. One night as we left an Anglican service of worship, Ali turned to me and asked, "What is the difference between a Methodist and an Anglican?" What irony! At a moment when I wanted to share my faith in Christ, I stood instead amid Buddhist and Hindu temples telling my Muslim friend about an eighteenth-century dispute and division that had absolutely no relevance or meaning in this cultural context. This incident reinforced my commitment to ecumenism and ensured my lifelong involvement in encouraging interreligious relationships. How often I have prayed for the vision of a uniting church in a divided world that acknowledges "There is one body and one Spirit . . . one Lord, one faith, one baptism, one God and Father of all" (Ephesians 4:4-6 NRSV). So indeed "that the world might believe" (John 17:21 NRSV).

Dialogue represents an expression of love to God and neighbor, caring enough to engage in an exploration for understanding. It is not a secret weapon or propaganda tool, but a way to reduce barriers and move fences. Only through dialogue can persons of differing perspectives transcend divisions sufficiently so they can labor together for mutual purposes. Reflective action, not just intellectual contemplation, emerging from dialogue can lead to steps to stop suffering, oppression, and death.[7] It can lead to the "abundant life" promised by Christ Jesus that we want for all God's people.

HISTORIC AND CONTEMPORARY PROPENSITIES FOR DISUNITY

Christians have been inconsistent in their quest for unity and goodwill toward others. Glen Messer and Benjamin Hartley have documented from historical research that John Wesley failed to fulfill at times the "catholic spirit" he proclaimed, citing his "less than charitable remarks" toward various groups, including Roman Catholics. Hartley and Messer also note differing theological notions of the nature of the church that question institutional unity as either a historical reality or a desirable theological end.

Even those who embrace ecumenism often quarrel among themselves, unwilling to recognize the validity of each other's clergy, traditions, and practices. When the World Council of Churches gathers, they cannot celebrate Holy Communion together. How can Christians expect the world to listen to our witness for justice, peace, and the integrity of creation, and against hunger, war, and environmental degradation, when we cannot agree to share the Lord's Supper among ourselves? Reportedly, a Muslim had to control the key to the Church of the Holy Sepulchre in Jerusalem for many decades because the Christian bodies that shared the sanctuary believed their fellow Christians would lock them out. Everywhere we need Christians who will imitate the spirit of Pope John XXIII, who said, "Whenever I see a wall between Christians, I try to pull out a brick."[8]

When the five-hundredth anniversary commemorating the beginning of the Protestant Reformation is celebrated in 2017, how do we recognize the contribution of that disunity and yet also not condone "the hatred, animosity, and bloodshed that followed"? Wesley Granberg-Michaelson reports there are an estimated 43,800 Christian denominations in the world, saying this astonishing number "indicates the growing complexity, enormous diversity, and proliferating disunity of world Christianity."[9] In the twenty-first century how do we find our unity in Christ without ever more splintering, separating, and schism?

Since at least 2004 some United Methodists have argued for "amicable separation" of the denomination. Recently the drumbeat of division has escalated, as despair about engaging in dialogue has intensified.[10] What divides United Methodists currently are not issues related to the doctrine of the Trinity or even Christology, but whether the church will celebrate same-sex marriages and include gay, lesbian, bisexual, and transgender persons (LGBT) at all levels of the church's life. If The United Methodist Church endorses schism— just as its predecessors once did over issues of race—there will be high costs and consequences impacting the global membership and mission of the church.

In the evolving debate, at least five approaches have emerged. Citing Bishop Scott Jones of Kansas, journalist Heather Hahn outlines the options this way:

- Enhance the ability of congregations and clergy who support same-sex unions to leave the denomination with their assets and benefits, while increasing consequences for violating the *Book of Discipline*'s stance.
- Let local churches decide—after a discernment process and super-majority vote—whether to host same-sex unions and welcome gay clergy.
- Empower annual conferences to make decisions on all matters not restricted by the denomination's constitution.
- Replace the current five, regionally defined U.S. jurisdictions with two ideologically defined jurisdictions and letting annual conferences vote on which jurisdiction to join.
- Amend the *Book of Discipline* to allow full inclusion of lesbian, gay, bisexual, transgender, and queer individuals
- Enable amicable separation into one or more denominations.[11]

In this book pastor Adam Hamilton addresses one of these alternatives, offering the contemporary United Methodist Church a path forward, as theological and political pressures toward schism threaten the institutional unity of the denomination. He pleads for a compromise in church polity position that might preserve the church's unity. By definition, a compromise can never match what everyone considers desirable, but only that which at the moment appears feasible.

The purpose of this book is not to endorse a particular route to maintaining unity, but to encourage continued conversation on the uncharted path of dialogue. Hamilton's perspectives and proposals illustrate anew the timeless and timeliness of the challenges ever facing the quest for Christian unity.

Christians realize that no longer can monologue pretend to be the language of God's loving and liberating mission of ministry. Our God is a God of dialogue, seeking to hear and heal the world's wounded and to share the abundant grace of life and love. We are instructed by the dialogic teaching style of Jesus that responded to a person's greatest fears and confronted people at their deepest levels of spiritual and human need. Recognizing the high costs and consequences of our propensity for disunity, we are summoned to engage in intensive dialogue and also hear Maxie Dunnam, chancellor of Asbury Theological Seminary, when he writes:

> Christ cannot give us unity if we are not willing to receive his grace and the unity that is his gift to the church. Could it be that this can come only through prayer and fasting?[12]

FOSTERING CHRISTIAN UNITY AND INTERRELIGIOUS RELATIONSHIPS

Individual Christians in their daily living are on the frontier of fostering Christian unity and interreligious relationships.

Ecumenical councils and formal interfaith dialogues do need to occur, but the real test is how persons of faith relate to one another in their families, workplaces, neighborhoods, clubs, and communities. Except perhaps those who live behind guarded gates or in homogeneous enclaves, most of the world no longer lives isolated from people of different religious traditions and perspectives. Almost all Christian families are interdenominational, and many of us cherish and honor loved ones who follow other world religions.

Bishop Hee-Soo Jung outlines in his chapter how United Methodists in the Chicago area have been intentional in creating interreligious relationships. Their "Declaration of Relationship" with Muslims is a model document that could be duplicated with other religious groups. Their unique interfaith bus trips immersed United Methodists in the faith communities of Jews, Jains, Sikhs, Buddhists, Hindus, and Muslims. As he notes, "the landscape of the religious field around us becomes noticeably interconnected as more families relate through interreligous marriages and adoptions."

People no longer necessarily remain in the religious tribe of their family. Thus I regularly share Shabbat with my Jewish daughter, son-in-law, and grandchildren. Hanukkah has become part of my December tradition along with Christmas. Friends call from India to seek counsel when their son marries into a Hindu family. United Methodist pastors may have Mormon or Muslim spouses. Ecumenical and interfaith issues are not esoteric, intellectual questions reserved for bishops, ecumenical officers, and academics. Rather it is the grassroots life of laity and clergy in today's world. To use colloquial language, it is where the rubber meets the road!

Pastors and local churches might audit themselves to see how hospitable we are in the language we use and the practices we observe. Sometimes, because of the love language we use honoring

Jesus, we make statements that exceed what we want to claim in the presence of persons of other faiths, or that may even denigrate another's beliefs or practices. Our United Methodist policies around Holy Communion are welcoming, inviting everyone to share in the Lord's meal, but sometimes pastors use excessively exclusivist language around the sacrament of baptism. As if only baptized Christian children were going to heaven!

Likewise as we go forward, many church members especially in the United States and Europe may find they are more and more outside their comfort zones if the denomination continues to proclaim that "The United Methodist Church does not condone the practice of homosexuality and considers this practice incompatible with Christian teaching."[13] Friends and family members may ask whether this more reflects bigotry and/or disrespect for human rights than a winsome witness of Christ's inclusive love for all people. Clearly this issue has emerged globally as a major stumbling stone for Christian unity and perhaps interreligious relationships in our time.

The spiritual work of maintaining Christian unity and augmenting interreligious relationships never ends. As a denomination, we expect our episcopal leaders and others to speak forthrightly and boldly through official offices and channels, like the Office of Christian Unity and Interreligious Relationships. Our theological seminaries must be preparing pastors who are ecumenists and are conversant with fostering interreligious relationships. United Methodists should promote bilateral dialogues with Roman Catholics, Lutherans, Mennonites, and other Christian communions. We are called to address racism and strengthen our participation in the Pan-Methodist Commission. We must continue our support for the World Council of Churches, the World Methodist Council, and national council of churches in every country where we serve. We need to find new ways of relating to Evangelicals, Pentecostals, Orthodox, and indigenous

Christian groups. We must never fear repenting for our sinful errors or seeking reconciliation whenever the opportunity arises, trusting in the leading of the Holy Spirit.

Speaking the truth in love and celebrating God's inclusive love in Christ Jesus remain at the heart of our Christian life and witness as we seek to foster the gifts of Christian unity and inter-religious relationships. As we pursue justice, equality, peace, and an abundant life for all, we will continue to affirm to others the words of John Wesley that "if your heart is as my heart, give me your hand."

QUESTIONS

1. How is the quest for Christian unity and interreligious relationships both timeless and timely?

2. How can we be dialogians of the faith in our daily living—with our families, friends, coworkers, and church?

3. Is schism inevitable in The United Methodist Church due to disagreements among members about same-sex marriage and issues related to lesbian, gay, bisexual, and transgender persons?

4. Can dialogue be effective in keeping United Methodists together?

5. What steps will you and your church take to foster Christian unity and interreligious relationships?

NOTES

1. Martin Luther King, Jr., *Where Do We Go from Here: Chaos or Community?* (New York: Harper & Row, 1967).

2. Ibid., pp. 167, 171.

3. Ibid., p. 190.

4. This section uses material previously published in Donald E. Messer, *A Conspiracy of Goodness: Contemporary Images of Christian Mission* (Nashville: Abingdon Press, 1992), pp. 138–39.

5. See Donald E. Messer, "Ecumenical Movement," *Contemporary American Religion*, Volume 1, Wade Clark Roof, editor in chief (New York: Macmillan Reference USA, 2000), pp. 215–17. Also Leonard Swidler, "Death or Dialogue: From the Age of Monologue to the Age of Dialogue," Grand Valley Review: Volume 6: Issue 2, Article 16.

6. Lesslie Newbigin, *The Open Secret: An Introduction to the Theology of Mission* (London: SPCK, 1978), p. 211.

7. Cited from Messer, *Conspiracy of Goodness*, p. 141.

8. Pope John XXIII, https://wau.org/resources/article/re_they_are _our_brethren/.

9. Wesley Granberg-Michaelson, "The Pilgrimage of Ecumenism: A Post-Christian West and the Non-Western Church," unpublished address, January 24, 2012.

10. See Amy Frykholm, "Covenant and Schism in the UMC: A Time to Split?" *The Christian Century*, April 16, 2014.

11. Heather Hahn, "Bishop: Beware of Costs of Sexuality Debate," http:// www.umc.org/news-and-media/bishop-beware-of-costs-of-sexuality -debate.

12. Maxie Dunnam, "Prayer and Fasting: Embracing Voluntary Weakness," *We Confess*, Newsletter of the Confessing Movement, July-September 2014, p. 3.

13. *The Book of Discipline of The United Methodist Church* (Nashville: The United Methodist Publishing House, 2012), ¶161.F, p. 111.

CPSIA information can be obtained at www.ICGtesting.com
Printed in the USA
LVOW10s0914190415

435102LV00002B/2/P